.

WATCHING
EVIL DEAD

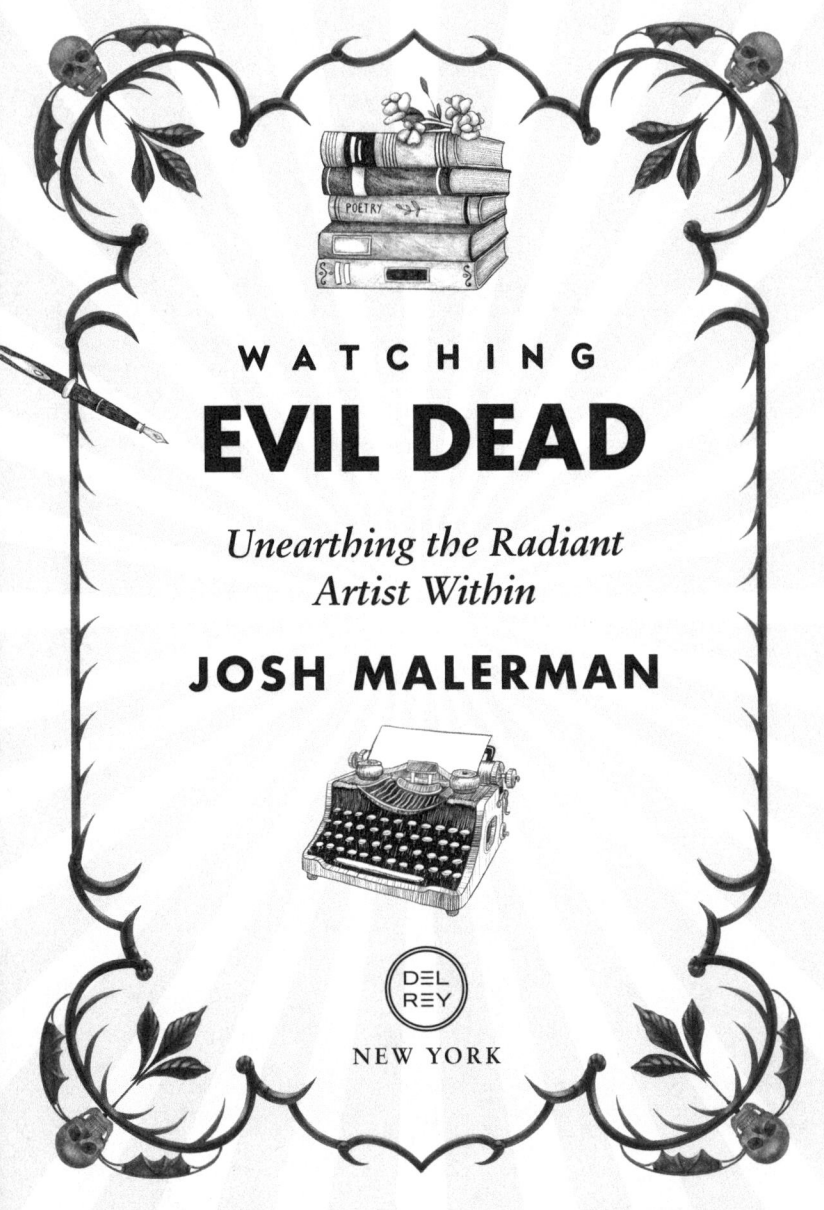

WATCHING
EVIL DEAD

Unearthing the Radiant Artist Within

JOSH MALERMAN

DEL
REY

NEW YORK

Del Rey
An imprint of Random House
A division of Penguin Random House LLC
1745 Broadway, New York, NY 10019
randomhousebooks.com
penguinrandomhouse.com

Hardback ISBN 978-0-593-98327-0
Ebook ISBN 978-0-593-98328-7

Printed in the United States of America on acid-free paper

2 4 6 8 9 7 5 3 1

First Edition

BOOK TEAM: Production editor: Cindy Berman • Managing editor: Paul Gilbert • Production manager: Angela McNally • Copy editor: Rachelle Mandik

Adobe Stock illustrations: Title page, Graficriver (starburst background), natalia (gothic frame), Luna Calderón (vintage typewriter), scarlet_heath (vintage books and pen)

Book design by Diane Hobbing

The authorized representative in the EU for product safety and compliance is Penguin Random House Ireland, Morrison Chambers, 32 Nassau Street, Dublin D02 YH68, Ireland, https://eu-contact.penguin.ie.

This book is for anyone who's ever had
a revelation mid-party and woken up
the next morning to discover it
wasn't just the punch talking.

WATCHING
EVIL DEAD

SEX IN A HOLY PLACE

ALLISON AND I ARE STILL just falling in love when she tells me she hasn't seen *The Evil Dead*.

I'm not the kind of cowboy who judges anybody on what they have and have not seen. If you're short on travel, drugs, sex, or art, you'll likely make up for it in the coming years. Maybe you'll even overcompensate. Some courses are fun to overcorrect.

We've all got gaps. Inexplicable holes in our history of movie-watching, book-reading, band-knowing, and painting-seeing. Who cares why? Most gaps aren't the result of planting a dogmatic flag in the sand; usually they're just there . . . because. But gaps are fun. Because, come one ordinary night, with no indication of anything special in the sky, you find yourself *filling* one. You're suddenly, spontaneously experiencing a work of art long lauded by the people you trust. You're inside it now, finally, living the legend, packing dirt into the gap that's forever marred your lawn. More often than not, you get why the thing was praised so highly and for so long. The real thrill, though, is this: you're so entranced by the work itself, you don't ask yourself what took you so long.

You just enjoy it.

Who cares if you're late to the party?

You're partying. Put a hat on.

Consider: there was once a day I didn't know what the word *fork* meant. Mom or Dad taught me, and from that moment forward I owned the word. When I use the word today, nobody accuses me of having once been ignorant. Art is no different. The seventy-year-old woman who reads Faulkner for the first time knows him as well as the seventy-year-old who read him at twenty. Once you fill the gap, there's no sign of fresh grass or a recently filled hole. Whatever you learn, whatever you experience, no matter when it occurs, it's then yours; you then own it. The same goes for what you create: If you don't make a movie till you're sixty? You're every bit the filmmaker as someone who started at sixteen. That's true even if you wanted to make a movie all those years but just never got around to it. That's true even if you were too scared, too broke, too bereft of ideas, too occupied with existence. It's also true if the notion had never crossed your mind, not once, in those sixty years prior to you suddenly wanting to do it and then seeing that desire through.

If you want to be an artist, you gotta finish works of art.

Once you do, you are.

And because all art is subjective (you don't need anyone to tell you that), it doesn't matter if what you create is *good* or *bad*. These words aren't truths. No more than intelligence can be measured by how much you know. Like the fork example. What you learned yesterday is as much yours as it is anybody else's. There is no *when* in the artistic life, only *before* and *after*. Before: you hadn't done it. After: you have. And so now . . . you *are*. What you want and what you do, these are the Pillars of You. Go find a dictionary of rare words and learn a few and use the words tomorrow. And the first person who asks if you just learned the word, you tell them, "*Eudaemonia* is just as much mine as *spoon*." Then you tell them *eudaemonia* is the contentedness you feel when broadening your horizons.

Maybe it'll inspire them to do just that.

And now that word is yours. And mine too. One day maybe I'll use it in a book.

So, when Allison tells me she hasn't seen *The Evil Dead*, all I see is the potential for a viewing party. I imagine the two of us sitting on the one piece of furniture we have in the small apartment we share: a faux-stylish white love seat thing I mistook for minimalism and later learned was more "antisocial monk who'd taken a vow of silence." The apartment was already monkish when I'd met Allison: a single end table, two orange lamps, two oval mirrors on the wall, a box of six horror soundtracks, and an army cot I called a bed. I had just enough money to pay for the place, but nowhere near enough to fill the two tiny rooms. I met my agent, Kristin Nelson, for the first time in that apartment, via Zoom or whatever it was called in those days, and I wondered if she was taking note of the empty space behind me. Did she think I was a minimalist? Well, I'm sure she drew her own conclusion when, after she asked who I banked with, I told her I'd kept all my money in a hardcover copy of *The Witches of Eastwick*.

I'd written some fourteen books by the time I met Allison Laakko, but I hadn't shopped one. Hadn't been accepted or rejected. Didn't know where to begin and anyway believed I'd already begun by writing the books themselves. There was a growing stack of rough drafts, enough of them that I kept them in an old wooden crate, this crate being one of only three items in the second small room of that little apartment. I wrote half of those books while riding in the passenger seat of the tour van for my band, the High Strung, some freehand, some not. I was (and still am) in a band with my best friends, who toured the United States and Canada for some 250 shows a year for close to six and a half years. We played to an average of twenty people a night. If you multiply the number of shows (close to 1,625) by twenty, you get one hell of a crowd. Over 30,000 people. As our drummer Derek Berk once said, "We didn't play stadiums . . . we played *stadium*." But even without the math, I found the nightly numbers fantastic, and so who could fault me for feeling fulfilled? And who could fault me for having no plan for the books when I was singing songs in a different city every night, getting paid in pizza and booze?

Yet, I did carry with me fantasies, delusions perhaps, in

which I'd debate story changes with fictitious editors, have imaginary interviews as if faced with *The New York Times*. I imagined the books, all of them, on a shelf, all lined up, each with a solid, scary spine. You could say I believed it would all come to pass, I just had no idea how something like that occurred.

But an incredible thing happened soon after I met Allison at a rock show in Michigan: I got a book deal. Kristin sold a book of mine called *Bird Box* to HarperCollins as part of a two-book deal.

And while I floated in the ecstatic waters of fresh love and first success, I also had my first revelatory inner insistence, a knocking on an inner door, a door deep within myself, on the other side of which stood a small, faceless man wearing an overcoat in the fog, a man who used the voice I always hear in my head when he asked:

Exactly what does an artist deserve?

A simple question. Or so I thought then. The answer wouldn't come for some time. And like most deceptively enormous inquiries, it started quiet, then got loud.

It would reach a profound volume the night Allison and I watched *The Evil Dead*.

For the time being: new love and a book deal. And if I didn't see things in potentialities before, I was now seeing every potentiality at once. It was overwhelming, but what was happening was so blatantly positive, I didn't bend or suffer beneath its weight. Love and books. Some money, too, a thing I hadn't had much of in close to twenty years.

Or ever, really. Music, too, as the band continued to play live shows without the incessant touring, a string of debaucherous local gigs during which I popped pot brownies onstage, raised bottles of Jack to the audience, and was once carried home by my brothers after falling into another band's drum set. I was waking up with headaches in those days, of course, but with the doctrine that I couldn't let a hangover stop me from my day's writing. That wasn't allowed. One of the many rules I'd followed for close to ten years. Because writing was never a hobby, not even when I did it for no reason (and had no prospects) other than to tell a story.

New love and books. And a hard, crazy respect for both.

I learned early that one can remain a gentleman while delivering the most grotesque of scenarios on the page, just like a married couple can honor each other while tying each other to the bed. Love . . . and the act of writing like the act of love. Equally electrifying and just as frightening. Ecstasy (and a sense of danger) to be found every day, every session, every time the mere *thought* of writing occurs.

Reverence, I discovered, for both. And wherever the twain shall meet. Because they do meet sometimes. In folded corners of practice, the far side of writerly rooms.

Or even in a landmark building in your hometown.

Here:

Allison tells me she's never seen *The Evil Dead*. We've already had a couple blundering nights in which we showed each other movies we thought were guaranteed to blow the other's mind but failed to do so. But tastes change. And who cares if the woman you fell for didn't laugh during *Raising Arizona*? It's all about timing. Or can be. And besides, the glass through which you observe art sure doesn't have to be the same pane used for your worldview. It's good to switch eyepieces, a monocle for this, a monocle for that.

And if there's one thing Allison has, it's a great collection of lenses.

Still, I'm thinking Allison's gonna like *The Evil Dead*. She certainly already knows about the guys who made it: Sam Raimi and Bruce Campbell grew up not four miles from the house we'll one day buy together, after the movie of my novel *Bird Box* gets made. These men aren't only Michiganders but metro-Detroiters. And most interestingly for now: they had an office back when, on Nine Mile Road in Ferndale. The same city in which Allison and I met.

It once was the city of Ferndale, Michigan, wasn't much more than a vibe. Adult theaters and massage parlors come with shadows and alleys, and it must have been hard for the *Evil Dead* guys to imagine it would one day become an epicenter for artists, alternative lifestyles, food, music, shopping. But blackout-drunk nights and bar fights will remain. Years after Allison sees *The Evil Dead,* she will shove a man to the sticky floor of a popular bar, a man who just punched me out in the back hall the night I signed the book deal for *Unbury Carol* with Del Rey Books. I'll see this takedown from the floor. I'll be smiling, my teeth covered in blood, when I do.

But long before then, and shortly after I got the book deal for *Bird Box,* Allison and I enter that old office building where the *Evil Dead* guys made their first calls, tried to sell their first movie. Me, I think I know which office was theirs. The city is hopping this day. It usually is. We stop in the Library Bookstore first because it's one of my favorite stores. We crouch in the horror section. We talk about how great the cover art was in the '80s. I introduce Allison to the bookseller, Denny, a man I once called from the road with the band, crouched in a different horror section in a used bookstore in Denver, Colorado, to ask if I should buy an anthology called *Dark Forces.* He said yes. In Ferndale, we chit, we chat, and Allison and I are floating. New love. We float out of the bookstore, up the sidewalk, on the wind of a city that's growing faster than the locals even know. Still, despite the endless stimulation, this old brick building stands out. There's something regal, something firm, something *original* in its bones.

Occultists talk about residual energy. Ghosts, perhaps, or tragedy, and comedy, and their resultant emotions, trapped. I like this idea. Maybe the energy, the timing, the bravery it takes to make a masterpiece leaves a little something behind too.

"Up here," I say, leading the way up an older stone staircase to the second floor. I say I *think* I know which one was

Sam and Bruce's office, but I'm not sure. That doesn't matter. It was somewhere in this building. And we're in this building now too.

The old wood floor creaks as we walk to the end of the hall. We stand before a wood door with frosted glass.

"I have to pee," Allison says.

The door's locked anyway. How long can we stare at the door? Well, maybe awhile anyway. Years later Allison and I will visit two of Anne Rice's homes in New Orleans. And while it's quickening, being close to where it happened, there's only so much you can actually do in someone else's space.

"Bathroom," Allison says. "Think it's this way."

I follow her back the way we came. Luckily, the bathroom's unlocked. The rest of the building is empty. We think.

We enter together.

Allison's in the stall while I'm at the sink, looking at the glass.

"Think they peed in here?" I ask.

"I don't think they peed in their office."

"True. True."

I'm seeing me in the mirror, in this building, wearing a button-up dress shirt, a black suit coat, a brown hat. I'm thinking of *Bird Box* being with HarperCollins. I'm thinking about the rewrite notes I'm supposed get back soon. It'll be the first real rewrite I've ever done. What reason would I have had to do any rewriting before? If you're not thinking of shopping your work, if you have no idea what that process entails, why not just write another book? And another after that?

I have vague visions of the cover art for *Bird Box*. I wonder if it'll resemble the covers we just drooled over at the bookstore up the street. I wonder what the font will be. The page count. The author photo. These are some of the magical elements of all books, but I'm starting to feel a little weird suddenly. Maybe it's because we're in the building where one of the biggest, most successful horror movies began. Maybe that's got me thinking of what comes next, for *Bird Box,* for me. I hear another knock on that inner door . . . the faceless man in the overcoat out in the fog . . . his lips parting to ask exactly what an artist deserves . . .

"Hey," Allison says, out of the stall now. "Let's do it in here."

What?

"What?"

Maybe the knock I heard inside me was the stall door closing after all.

All thoughts of books and careers are obliterated. Allison is unbuttoning my shirt.

I think to say, *Wait;* I think to say, *Hold on, we should check.* But ultimately I land on: "Okay. Amazing. Yes."

And it is amazing. We're not just having sex in a public place; this is the *Evil Dead* building.

We could be facing the same mirror the *Evil Dead* guys used. And we're not thinking about the undead.

Well, maybe I am a little bit.

"You hear that?" I ask.

But Allison doesn't even look to the door.

This is unbelievable for a few reasons. It feels like we're turning our backs on more than decorum; we can't stop falling in love any more than I could ever stop writing and I'm realizing this, in this building, I'm realizing I have a partner in facing the future, something that's recently become even more unknown than usual. We're acting like high schoolers (awesome), and it strikes me I've always felt a little like a high schooler, always felt bizarrely *young,* and maybe writing books and falling in love is the fountain of youth. I'm thirty-seven years old when I meet Allison and get the book deal a few months later. What is age then? When are you too old to sneak into the cemetery after dark? When are you too old to write the book you've always believed you had in you? The answers are so obvious, here, there, in the bathroom of the *Evil Dead* building. But why are these answers harder to spot in the world at large?

"This is incredible," I say.

It feels like we're somewhere other than a bathroom. It feels like we're having sex in a pocket of existence where you can speak things into being. Not so much manifestation as . . .

"Momentum," I say.

Yes. That's the word. I'd written in a vacuum for nearly twenty years. No author friends, no publishing-house contacts, no circle of readers. I'd spent close to ten of those years failing to finish a novel. I'd tried four times. Then, following *Wendy* (my first, finished), a decade of title after title, draft after draft, a stack of pages taller than myself, enough to fill a crypt, a casket full of rough drafts, and now, here, one of those books was *going to be published.*

What's age, what's timing, what's history to the storyteller? What's age to the unknown artist, the artist within, the one who will emerge the same way desire does? If it's in you, it's gotta get out. And when it does . . . What's time? What's place?

You own the words you learn. They are eternally yours. But you *possess* the works of art you finish. And as those works spread as they are read, so do you.

Momentum . . .

Here I stand . . . thirty-seven . . . still new to this woman who has pulverized my anxieties, my hang-ups that appear so silly to me now. Allison the artist, singer, athlete, thinker. A personality so rare, everyone who's known her knows she is an island, a solo, and here I've met her, heard her, a courtship so intense I lost twenty pounds throughout, visibly changed by her, as I understood, in full, immediately, this is the person I was going to be with, going to listen to albums with, read books with, watch movies with, grow old with too. Hark: horror, art, love, sex, confidence. And not just the breaking of rules, but the beginning of seeing a world without many rules at all.

There's the spirit of art, of course. In Allison, in the courtship. And the now obvious motivations for taking on specific projects. And the reasons for seeing them to completion. Because being with Allison feels the same to me as being with a new book idea; the rush within, the way the excitement rises up, the way, when you're near the person you love or you're carrying around an idea you know you're going to write, you feel smarter, funnier, sharper.

People say you should be with someone who brings out the best in you. And it's true. And it's true of art, as well.

Momentum . . .

Still in the bathroom, still having sex, I'm thinking of a potential night in which we watch *The Evil Dead* and maybe she'll like it, maybe she won't, and who cares so long as I'm near her, so long as we can hear each other gasp, laugh, breathe. Because already I'm finding less meaning in things when Allison isn't there. You don't really know how micro you can get, how small a thing can be, a thing you wanna share, until you've been netted by the maddest of love. A night at the opera, okay; a road trip, of course; a flight, a reunion, all that, yes yes. But what you really want is for that person to have been there when the credit card machine at Walgreens made a funny sound. When the aisle of paper towels is so overstuffed it looks like a padded cell and you play inmate for her. You wanna joke with that person. You wanna experience the interstitials, the threads that hold the set-piece photo ops together. Every moment seems to be leading to the next, giant stones crossing a loud river, rocks of art and lust, easy to step on, so powerful to cross.

Who could possibly take seriously the words *good* and *bad* under these conditions? Who could possibly hear platitudes or blanket statements when in the throes of such a layered, complex, rich experience?

Our cherished artists, they've all made lemons. They've all made stuff we don't love. The key is to make no demarcation between yourself and the voice on the radio, the picture on the back of the book. Art is not the province of those who were born with an aptitude for art. You are an artist too. So why fear failure? Of any stripe?

Momentum!

(Allison and I, still facing the mirror the *Evil Dead* guys maybe once faced.)

Momentum!

Momentum creates the steady, consistent motion of the writer's life. How a person can be "in writing shape" just like running shape, just like reading shape too. A novella can look daunting if you haven't read a book in three months, but an epic series is welcome if you've been eating books on the regular. It's all the same, reading and writing in these incremental installments, these daily-dos, and then, presto, *change*—in the form of an accomplishment. There's often a lot of debris between the writer and the written word, the idea and the rough draft. Lifting that debris out of the way, cleaning your room, that's what keeps a writer in writing shape. Intentionality feeds off intentionality. You keep the space clean, it's easier to write the book. You write the book, it's easier to believe you can write another one. Ad infinitum. I don't believe in writer's block. I only believe in being out of writing shape. There's a dance to the writer's life. And you gotta want to dance.

Consider: What better source of identity does an artist have than their finished works?

What better way to learn your real name?

"We're crazy," Allison says.

Sweet. Crazy. Both. It feels like we're starting a circus, opening a theater. Feels like, even in only each other, we've discovered the ringleaders for a circus, the MCs for a stage. And why not open a philosophical show? Is there not momentum to be found in the ripples cast by those with whom you share this life? When I met Allison, it felt like we'd agreed upon an open secret: yes, a show we'd bring with us wherever we went. There's a tightrope to walk in the circus, and sometimes you fall no matter how well you practiced. But if a life lived is its own body of work, and if in life and art you allow yourself the lemons even your heroes put out there, you begin not only to forgive yourself these moments of *less-than*, you start to see the humanity in them; you realize they make for a better show. And life.

Tightrope . . . falling . . .

But I bet the net feels good.

"Oh my God," Allison says. Or I say it. Or both.

Performance . . .

I played my first "show" at nineteen, with friends, some of whom, down the road, would become the High Strung, the band I'm still in today. The venue was a place in Ferndale called Gotham City Café. This place, not a mile from the building where the *Evil Dead* guys once tried to sell their film, remains fixed in my memory as a North Star. At nineteen, I didn't know how to speak about this life I was creating yet, how to write it, not even close. I missed significances all around me. Powerful, meaningful episodes passed over and under me; I wasn't equipped to *see* the artistic arc. This doesn't make that first show a bad one. In fact, it's more interesting for it. Because there was a whole naïveté to that period, and aren't "failures" and "successes" both born of an artist naïve to their own shortcomings?

Their abilities too?

Some people look for folly in all the art they experience. A lot of people like it. And some people judge others based solely on how much of this humanness they think they see in them. Authenticity, they say! But sincerity is both difficult to verify and easy to spot. Still, we know when we ourselves are sincere. And we see the effect our sincerity has in conversation, in interaction, in art.

Your path is so clear then, yes? Get into good-enough writing shape so that the *work* of it doesn't cross your mind—the hours, the toil, the deleting of a day's progress.

Get into good-enough writing shape to where you're not feeling the strain, the push, the pull. To where you have the energy to consider every conceit. Because it's in that place where you can be yourself, in full, *sincere,* without exerting the effort to do so. And the people with whom you've surrounded yourself (your friends, your peers, your love) will see and encourage your truth.

Allison and I stand still a moment in the bathroom of the *Evil Dead* building. Hard to move right away after that. We look at each other in the mirror and we laugh. We're pulling our pants up and we're laughing because this wasn't planned. No more than the next scene in a pantser's book. (Pantser: as in fly by the seat of your pants, write by the seat of your pants, rather than using a detailed outline. I'm definitely a pantser, with some landmarks written in Sharpie on the office walls and sudden revelations on Post-its all over the desk.)

"Quiet building," Allison says.

"I'm guessing it once wasn't."

"Well, now we *have* to watch the movie."

"Totally."

We hurry up and exit the bathroom and I think how perfect it would be for someone to climb the steps just then, to pop out of an office down the hall, having no idea of the events leading up to our encountering them.

Or maybe it's written all over us.

Sincerity.

On the walk home, Allison and I are glowing under the day sky. We just did something kinda wrong. A little crazy. Likely illegal. I'm hoping we did.

It feels like the entire world has opened up to me. Allison, *Bird Box,* the band. I'm thinner for the courtship, the excitement, the anticipation. I'm alert to all things bright, smart, alive. We see people we know, we stop to talk, we walk on. I can feel momentum coursing through me like whiskey. We walk the path. Ideas grow plantlike on all sides of the path. It feels like we turned the sun on ourselves.

But despite these wonders, despite this near overwhelming sense of potential, I hear that knock again. Way inside myself. It's that man outside in the fog with that question. The question that's come to me now a few times, which is a few times more than I'm prepared for. Do you hear similar questions asked at your inner door?

Exactly what does an artist deserve?

Bird Box is set to be published a year from this date, the date Allison and I have sex in a holy place. And what do I expect upon its publication? And what do I . . . deserve?

I take Allison's hand.

"I love you," I say.

But it feels like I said it just to block out that question. I sense a big answer in there. One that details expectations and desires, topics beyond good or bad, complicated stuff I'm not ready to ponder.

I wonder if this is why I want to introduce her to *The*

Evil Dead. Because that movie marked Sam Raimi's start. Ninety minutes of Sam Raimi taking his own first steps.

And what did he deserve?

But maybe I just wanna share something with Allison. Share everything. No matter how big or small.

So, *Not now,* I tell the faceless man knocking in the fog. *Come back later. We'll talk then. I promise.*

But he doesn't come back later.

He never really leaves.

PIVOTS ON A DIME

I DON'T PICK FAVORITES. CERTAIN BOOKS blaze, certain images burn, and certain songs sound sung from the outer rim. It has little to do with technicality and so much to do with courage, essence. I'm thinking of *Moby-Dick*, and the heat I felt while finishing it at the end of a dock in Michigan's Upper Peninsula. I'm thinking of *Tropic of Cancer* in a coffee shop in New York City, classical music loud in the house speakers; I'm physically breathless with the book's climax. I'm thinking of Poe, Proust, Whitman, Woolf. Writers of brio. Men and women who were able to transfer their spirit to the page, so that anybody who reads it, anytime, any era, will know it.

To possess the page . . .

Bird Box was one of the most fluid rough drafts of my life. Man, was it smooth. It was October of '06 and all I had was an image of a woman and two kids, blindfolded, navigating a river. I wrote between the hours of eight A.M. and noon and by nightfall of each day I knew what I was going to write the next day. No speed bumps with that draft. Zilch. Still, the rewrites were enormous. Eleven rounds, gloves off, including rewriting the entire novel from scratch (except the birth scene), this after HarperCollins had already picked it up. Did I possess the page with that story? Do we, every time? Well, yes and no. Goal or not, the silly part is trying to predict when these magic moments come. Some call it inspiration. Okay. That's fine. But inspiration is an inverted monster: rather than charging into your office, it waits outside the door, pressed flat to the hall wall, forcing the writer to wait, to procrastinate, fooling the writer into believing they need it before they can begin.

Get thee behind me, Inspiration.

Don't you know? If you write every day for a month, then read every day's writing, you'll have no idea which days were inspired and which were not? That's the beauty of the book. Naked Voice. There's no hiding *you* in a book. Whether you feel like writing or not, you are revealed. And so, without needing inspiration to begin . . . why not always . . . begin?

It's a revolving door, the daily sessions of the rough draft. And sometimes that spirit will step in with you and sometimes it won't. But these things can be fixed.

THERE IS NO BUDGET FOR WRITING A BOOK.

That's inspiration enough for me.

"And this," Allison says as we step into one of the upstairs bedrooms of the house we're looking to rent on Dunham Street in Ferndale. "This could be your office."

It's perfect. Nothing flashy. Dark-brown walls. A small

wood balcony overlooking the small city-sized backyard. This will be the first "office" I've ever had. Fourteen books deep, years of writing in band vans and bars, libraries and all-night diners. But here, my own space.

"I love it," I say. And I feel the tiniest flash of concern: *Will I still be myself in here? Will a room of my own change me?*

As grateful as I am for the room, it is change. And even horror authors must admit: nothing scares us quite as much as change.

I'm thinking of books as Allison and I leave the office-to-be and check out the rest of the upstairs. I'm thinking of bookshelves too. And where all our books will go. I'm thinking how I can locate the idea, the reason any book was written in the first place. It's something like empathizing with the authors, all authors. For this, I don't dismiss anything I read. What am I gonna do? Get angry at someone for not being any good at rolling their idea out? Naw. And I have no favorites. Key artists, of course, those who were fortunate enough to time that revolving door most often. And how much of that is luck? And how much does perpetual (but steady, smart) motion (momentum) increase the chances of striking artistic gold while also increasing the chances of writing a lemon, a thing we've already determined can reveal greatness and humanity too? I'm a sports fan, but I love the fact art isn't sport.

As Allison and I check out what will be our bathroom/shower for the next two years, I'm seeing all books as non-linear, as if they had all been released at once. What's a release date once the book is out in the world? I'm thinking how, a year from our first walk-through of the house, *Bird Box* will be as eternal as *The Old Man and the Sea,* as are all books, every one of them.

"Two showerheads," I say. "*Fancy.*"

Compared to the tiny apartment we've been living in, it *is* fancy. It's exhilarating. And the only reason I can afford it is because of the book deal.

That word comes up again . . . *deserve* . . .

I don't like it. Even as we're floating through potential futures, I find myself plucking this thorn from my paw. It's still vague. But while I don't fully grasp what I'm asking myself, I recognize it as something I'll need to eventually face.

"There's a walk-in attic," Allison says. "Maybe it can become an art space."

Allison the makeup artist, the painter, the special-effects artist. But while the stairs to the attic are wide enough to carry a couch, it's stuffy up there. Feels more like a costume trailer. It'll eventually be filled with clown wigs, varsity jackets from fictional towns, dresses splattered with fake blood. A shame, in a sense, because it seems like a real good place for a séance. A great setting for putting your eventual ghost on the page.

Consider: what's more occult than a book, any book, in which the writer has successfully transferred their spirit to the page?

"Ever think of books as residual energy?" I ask her as we discover small doors in the attic, big enough to crawl through, a pathway of sorts back there, so one could traverse the circumference of the attic, one door to the other. Sooner than later, this will become a party favor, a parlor trick, as we invite drunk guests upstairs and dare them to "circle the attic."

"Of course," Allison says. "Like music."

The same is true of movies, of course. And *The Evil Dead* is unquestionably one of the great examples, if not *the* great example, of capturing energy on film. Still . . . is it my favorite? I'm too experiential to pick favorites. Maybe it'll be my favorite the day we watch. Maybe not. In the days following Allison having told me she hasn't seen the movie, I'm not necessarily moving mountains to show her. But it is on my mind. I was writing a book called *Track & Field* in our last days at the apartment, the story of a track team that defies their new coach's demands and runs out to Mongrel Field, where they suddenly feel the urge to be wholly honest with one another. I'm seeing the correlation, of course, between the book and this sudden, new relationship. Every time one of the runners reveals themselves, I'm thinking of Allison, and how I don't want to hide anything from her, would never lie to her, would rather tell her every truth as it presents itself than wait for her to sense them on her own. Something is being established between us. We're not investigating each other's lives: we're sharing things before questions are even asked.

There's a fluidity previously unknown to me. As if we're listening to the audiobooks of each other's autobiographies.

And hers is incredible.

Allison paints and sometimes paints on the walls. I write notes for the books on the walls. Our little apartment became a work of art itself. So, as we walk through the house, I'm seeing the walls as canvases. I wish we could've brought the apartment walls with us to this house.

The whole world is like this now. There are canvases everywhere we look. This artistic life I've been living is getting wider, taller, more honest, more heated. I'm in love and I'm listening to Allison's autobiography and I'm stepping through that revolving door daily and sometimes the spirt makes it in and other times it doesn't. We couldn't take the walls with us, but the landlords of the little apartment sent me a note that we're gonna get the security deposit back because they always repaint the walls anyway. I can't help but think even the landlord felt it, this life, and decided to let it go.

There were outlines for books on those walls! Anthems, mottos, absurdisms. Scenes too. Years later I'll be writing about those walls, sitting between two newer outlines for two newer books on the walls of the office of the first home I'll ever buy. But that's a long way off. A long way from the night Allison finally watches *The Evil Dead*.

The first day we move into the house we're renting, Allison and I are walking around, saying *wow* over and over because there's more space than anyplace either of us has ever lived. We'll eventually film the climactic finale to an insane potty-humor movie we'll make very soon after the novel *Bird Box* is published. I'll need to make that movie because the book launch will feel frighteningly professional to me. I'm a guy, after all, who records albums on 4-track cassette decks, who played to an average of twenty people a night for more than six years, who will have written more than a dozen novels by the time *Bird Box* is released. I'll need to remind myself who I am. *Jizzly Bear* will do that, to say the least—a feature film I made with a band of lunatic friends, screened at the local art house. I'll need that movie the same way kids need to rebel against their parents. Only this will be me rebelling against myself. Some nights I'll even sleep on the floor of this house, just to remind myself where I come from.

But Allison and I were talking about a lot of things in those days: story ideas and song ideas and parties we'd like to throw, and which room should be the office and which the art room. We're living in a real neighborhood, and we've got a basketball net outside and some nights it feels like I could write an entire novel before the sun rises; the whole world is made up entirely of ideas. If I have a book idea, I add it to "The List" and I know I'll make good on it because the process is to go down the list, commit to each, to give all to each, and not take more than a couple months between big projects. I'm keeping in writer's shape, after all.

I'm seeing novels and songs as photo albums, snapshots of an artistic life, portraits of the artist steadily taken throughout the year, every year, so that I never look back and realize I haven't written in a decade and oh my God who is that looking back at me? That's the big fear. I imagine all prolifics feel this way. *Prolifics* as a noun. An artist who creates a lot. A prolific. I'm one. Partly from the horror of getting lazy. Of looking the other way too long and missing an idea. People tend to canonize the tortured artists, those who struggled to carve out their work. But there's no advantage between the optimists and the tortured souls, and if I can mostly remain the former, I'll take it. Writer's block doesn't come from a lack of ideas but from being out of writer's shape, and not having the energy, the stamina, to raise the idea like a child.

I've got new ideas in this new house. Immediately. So many it feels like my body could break apart with them.

Oh, it's electrifying. Any idea goes! Some of the plots for the greatest novels are tiny. What we love isn't the plot, the setting, the skill. We respect all that. But what we love is *character,* often including that of the writer, in action, the prism through which they see, the decisions they make, the lenses they look through: a monocle here, a monocle there.

Allison and I talk about these things. She's a perfectionist. I'm a lo-fi maverick. I'll take my chances. She won't. Together we'll do incredible things (maybe this balance/imbalance in process brings something out in each other), but in those early days I do wonder what the differences in our approaches mean. About us. About who we are. She's about as spontaneous a person as I know. Yet her art is curated, careful, exact. And while I could be a lot more spontaneous in ordinary life, I'm a split-decision-maker on the creation side: I'd write and release an album by sunrise if dared to do so. We have a lot to learn from each other, but in the early days you're not thinking of things like learning and lessons. You're just . . . together.

Turns out the extra bedroom becomes her art space. But in a way, the whole house does.

I used to think it'd be dangerous to fall in love with an artist. To date someone who came from the clouds, who spends as much time as I do up there . . . I used to think *one* of us needed a foot in reality. Who would ground us? If we're both made of helium, how would we stay tethered? What I didn't understand (in fact, I wholly missed it) was there's no reason to be grounded. No reason at all. No matter how far out you are, you're still experiencing the same dynamic reality as everyone you meet. So why not live in a house in the clouds? Why not you and I, aloft? There's a self-consciousness I've seen in musicians where we're embarrassed to try certain things. You've got your way of singing, this is how *you* do it, and so to sing any other way isn't *you*. It used to be I heard someone like Christina Aguilera on the radio and I'd think, "I would never try something like this." Yet, the truth is, I could never *do* something like she does. So why not try? And in falling short, in missing the mark, maybe I would add something to what I *could* do along the way. I'd likely come closer to what I want to do, my ideal, by trying things I don't consider *me*.

You usually write novellas? Try a 300,000-word book next. You love third person? Write the next in first. Or second. Or discover fifth on your own.

And so . . . Allison . . . a living work of art, a woman who paints, sings, acts, models, runs, plays classical guitar, plays piano, and writes. And it's not just what she does but who she is, and who she *obviously* is. Nobody's ever mistaken Allison for an everyday person. Whatever specialness she's got, it shines out of her eyes, her voice, her thoughts. I was a little scared when we first met. Scared of losing my foot in reality. But what are you gonna do when someone like this shows up unannounced? You're gonna follow her. And follow your heart. Every writer, every artist, has instincts, and those include matters of the heart. That idea you want to explore is like that human being you want to explore. And that colorful body of work you want so badly can be achieved by opening yourself up to things, and people, you didn't think were *you*. It didn't take long for me to sense a weightlessness with Allison. I could see the floor, the earth, the world getting smaller below us as we bounced ideas all night every night and fell into each other's art. It didn't take long for me to recognize there was never any foot and never any reality to begin with.

And it wasn't helium we were full of anyway.

Spirit. Will. Earnest fire! Allison and I want to be the best artists we can. For that we end up living the artist's life, intentionally, forcefully, or not. To us, this means seeing to completion any idea that touches a nerve, from those that trumpet a path to greatness to tiny ones that only give you a wink. Often it's those little thoughts that end up stretching the canvas, your canvas, your body of work and who you are. If the original idea thrills you at any point in time, even if only for less than a minute while doing laundry, write it down.

O! Momentum!

Some artists want to push the envelope. The great ones find out where to send the letter.

And to get there . . . we need to fail at mimicking singers who are nothing like us. We need to absorb the advice, the tricks, of fellow musicians. We need to write stories we hadn't planned on writing.

We need to embarrass ourselves.

Wear clothes that don't fit. Whine. Cry. Yell. Tantrum. We need to do what we think would be foolish, only to find that in falling short we're actually coming closer to being who we want to be, even if we once believed that ideal was out of reach.

And whose reach are we talking, here? Think of this sentence: *You're* not writing the book *you* believe *you* have in *you*. That's a lot of *you*s. Why not change one?

"Kenickie has a DVD of *The Evil Dead*," Allison tells me.

We're in the kitchen, opening and closing the refrigerator, blown away by how much room there is.

Kenickie is Allison's cousin. Blond and brash. Loud, smart, funny. Allison is nearly one hundred percent Finnish, and Kenickie seems twice that.

"Perfect," I say. "When?"

I'm already imagining a night of whiskey and grass. Cabins and demons. I have no idea what an understatement this is.

We talk dates. Times. I'm listening to her, watching her, this beautiful aria of a person in this gorgeous home. I'm thinking, suddenly, scared . . .

Do I deserve this?

This time the question arrives clarion, in such a clear voice, and I consider it. I've never been one to berate myself. I allow for lemons (you know), but I shoot for the moon too. I don't believe in "imposter syndrome." I think there should always be an officer on call to keep those two words apart. Still, the word *deserve* is its own complicated concept. An answer to the incessant question is in me, I can feel it, I know it's there. Like the faceless man outside the inner door, the man asking over and over: the answer is just as much there as he is. But why can't I simply answer this question or answer it simply? Have I answered it before? Is something in the way? Pride? Fear?

Why do I keep pushing this question away? Is it because I think the answer is obvious? Or do I detect a pivot, a new point of view, because of the ways in which my life has recently changed . . .

"He lives in Royal Oak," Allison says, talking about her cousin. "With his girlfriend, Rose."

What does an artist deserve . . .

I think again of the triviality of age, the madness of measuring accomplishment by age. But I didn't come to that conclusion on my own. Just like Mom taught me *fork* and the word became mine, Allison broke apart my ideas of age. We were sleeping on the army cot just outside the tiny kitchen of that small apartment with the writing all over the walls. We were listening to Paul McCartney and I said, "He still has a great voice."

And Allison asked, "Why wouldn't he?"

Now, Allison has an unbelievable voice, the kind that can sing any song, on any stage. From open mic to Broadway. The living room to the opera house.

"Well, he's like seventy or something," I said.

"We gotta stop being surprised when artists get better with age," she said. "We should expect that instead. Think of all the time they've spent doing what they do."

I lay there on that tiny cot, looking up. I wasn't thinking of an argument for what she'd said, because I didn't want to know one. She'd spoken a truth and I wanted to take that truth in. I pivoted then on a dime. I didn't tell her or anybody else that I needed time for her philosophy, her truth, to sink in. It immediately became my truth, my thinking. I brought up Hitchcock and how he was as old as the century. How most people would argue his peak came in his fifties, *Psycho* released when he was sixty-one. Without shame I completely championed the view she had taught me only seconds before. And then, it felt as if I *did* hold that view already. The High Strung didn't hit the road till we were twenty-seven. Well into our thirties we were playing dive bars filthy enough to make bikers reconsider, a different city every night, and loving every minute of it. But while I may have been living Allison's worldview, I was also younger then, and hadn't been tested by time, the duration of an artistic life. Did she hand me her worldview, a fresh one, exactly when I needed it?

Aspect, angle, attitude.

What a gift.

I've still got her present today. I entered the publishing world at age thirty-nine. Soon I'd be standing before *People* and *USA Today, The New York Times Book Review* and *Time* in the Museum of Modern Art in New York City, there to present *Bird Box,* a ten-foot poster of the book's cover like a castle's shadow behind me. Me, who had written in a vacuum for twenty years. Me, who had almost never performed for a group of people without my band. And here, at that museum and with that crowd, I stood before them and I felt *young.*

Yes! Young at heart and young in art. Rather than buckling under the weight of twenty years of working alone, I felt like it was day one. *Day one.* The birth of a career. And while I was scared out of my head (Allison told me to drink an airplane bottle of Jack from the hotel room before I headed to MoMA), I did not feel old. I did not feel past any window. I did not feel out of breath from the trip to this moment in time. What Allison taught me that day about the artist's journey changed my life.

Listen to those you trust. Study them. And don't be afraid to make immediate pivots in your philosophy when you hear a truth spoken, one you know is right, even if you'd opposed it a minute before. There's no shame in immediate acceptance.

I'm thinking about these things while Allison and I walk around the big house we're renting. We've got a bed now. I've got an office. There's a washer and a dryer. I'm reconsidering so many things as I walk from floor to floor. I'm coming up with story ideas in every room and I'm thinking, too, about the twenty years that led up to getting a book deal, and the lifetime that led up to meeting Allison. I'm thinking I wanna do something outrageously lo-fi to counter this semblance of commercial success, though *Bird Box* the book won't make the bestseller list for another four years, when the Netflix movie puts it there. I'm thinking I wanna do something absurd to balance the scales. Why do I feel this way? I don't know that answer. I keep the act of writing, all writing, in a safe place. I bring it out daily, I work, I play, it makes me laugh, it makes me crazy, I put it back. It's gotta go back in its case, safe from pressure, trends, brands, drugs, alcohol, love, distraction. In the early days, my agent, Kristin, sends me an email detailing publishing trends. Where the industry is heading. I don't read it. Not because I'm above these things, not because I don't care what an audience wants to read, but because a Spidey sense goes off anytime something with the potential to distort my feelings for writing gets too close. I don't read about the trends. Instead, I walk the house, thinking of what my friends and I can do here. I'm thinking of taking writing out of its box. To play.

While we're still in the kitchen, Allison says, "Kenickie says we should go watch it with him and Rose. Their place. This weekend."

And so the wheels are spinning. But they have been for a long time. And even I don't need the philosophy of a friend to tell me that much.

"This weekend. Sweet," I agree. It's settled.

We're going to watch *The Evil Dead* at Kenickie and Rose's house.

There will be whiskey, there will be grass. Who knows what else?

There will be a movie that captured the spirit of its creator.

It all feels occult. Wiccan. Like we're dabbling in magic whether we know the spells or not.

You can feel these things. The winds of witches coming.

Sounds like a great night waiting to happen.

Turns out to be more. Turns out to be legendary.

LEAP TO A LANDING, THEN LEAP AGAIN

I GRADUATED FROM MICHIGAN STATE UNIVERSITY in the late '90s. It's where Mark Owen and I started writing songs together before we officially started the High Strung in New York City. East Lansing is where I tried to write my first novel. I made it three hundred pages into *A Silo Maid* but didn't know how to finish back then. It's where the band started playing. Derek, Berko, Mark, me. It's where I got arrested for a noise violation. It's where we hosted LSD parties, even if I only drank Southern Comfort instead.

Michigan State was home to a thousand firsts for me and my friends.

Betsy Baker wears a Michigan State sweatshirt in the first *Evil Dead*.

For Spartans who love horror, this is gold.

But it's also become prescient, for me, in hindsight.

A class that changed me was outside my major, and I took it only because a bandmate, Jason Berkowitz (Berko), raved about the professor. Andrew Barclay taught phenomenological psychology, a subject I knew nothing about. Some days it felt like Barclay knew nothing about it, either, as he sat in a chair at the base of the auditorium (students came to Barclay's lectures who weren't enrolled in his class) and went chaotically deep into subjects that seemingly had nothing to do with psychology or even school. But that was his aim: Phenomenological psychology is about the experience itself, as opposed to any predetermined, static notions. It asks us to find meaning and explanation in the immediate world, rather than by way of ledgers, rules, or yesterday's results. To me, this felt like someone was saying: Never mind the details, never mind the current thinking, follow no trends: *be you now*. But be mindful about it, aware, enough so that you get from experiences (all experiences) answers, whether those answers are inevitable or not. Barclay's lectures were events, ones in which I was required only to be present, to be mindful, to *be*.

And the feelings I got in that lecture hall carried over, went back with me to the house we all shared, where the band practiced, where Mark and I were writing albums, where we were all falling in love with art. I'd never paid much attention to details anyway—I'd taught myself the guitar—but now, nudged by Barclay's example, I was stepping off the ledge, sensing a world of possibilities through an experientialist's lens.

Mark and I felt this influence immediately. Why not write a song outside our comfort zone, so long as it added to the group of songs, the album, the growing body of work? By pointing out the experience itself, Barclay had pointed out the journey: I was discovering the canon, the oeuvre, the body of work. Things changed for me. My approach to art especially: Whenever I read a book I liked, I read everything by that author. I watched entire filmographies. I listened to entire discographies. My lens widened: from song to album to career. And with it, less pressure on each song, each album, and (eventually) a career of my own. As I worked through the full careers of wholly different artists, I discovered what really turned me on was the idea of *phases,* the changes, and the freedom to switch unannounced from one style to another. I became mindful of the *experience* of writing. Did it matter how many people were at our shows? How much we'd get paid? And, later, how many albums we'd sold?

I'm able now to take stock of where this philosophy brought me: The band's never had a "Pour Some Sugar on Me" moment. We've never had a billion-copy bestselling song or album. And while we did write/record the theme song to Showtime's *Shameless,* none of our albums really outshone the others in any material way. That said, none of them did any less either. I think now of the circus atmosphere in Barclay's lectures. Standing room only, young men and women revering the professor like a fabled stage actor. He was connecting with us on a primitive level, albeit through an intellectual delivery. Recently I heard a podcast in which three people were ranking the albums of the High Strung. At some point they agreed that, if they didn't know better, they wouldn't be able to put the albums in chronological order. But what does this mean exactly?

To me: It means we're still focused on the same things now as we were when we started. Or, rather, we're still *not* focused on the same things we've always been not focused on. And why this works is, had we been concerned with money or celebrity, we would've stopped when neither arrived. If those were the goals, the destination, we'd have changed course long ago. Instead, we've prioritized the experience. Without ever saying so. It's not like we had a band meeting in which we laid down what we wanted out of this. But birds of a feather—and Allison and I are the same—flocked together . . .

It's the same thing with the books. It's been one giant phenomenological experience from the get-go. Words like *momentum* have become shorthand for those dreamish lectures Andrew Barclay once delivered, as if all of life was and is a psychological thriller.

Our night watching *The Evil Dead* became all these things, distilled. As if our entire lives had been leading up to that evening. A seemingly simple night in. Friends and a movie. A home near our own. And who can predict when these nights will come? And in what form?

The first time I meet Kenickie is at Allison's aunt and uncle's place in Birmingham, Michigan. It's also the first time I meet Allison's parents. I'm nervous as hell. Sweating nervous. Allison and I are still new. Before we met, I'd been single for some five years, but Allison was going on only four months. There's a side of me that wants to give her room, worries this whirlwind is happening too soon for her. For me it's perfect timing. I haven't thought of dating in years. I'm playing in the band, writing novels, hanging with a brilliant group of people, drinking like wedding guests wherever we go. I'm writing, I'm reading, I'm broke. So when Allison and I meet . . . it feels like there's her, there's me, yes, but there's also Timing. We talk about that a lot in those early days; we both know this is a permanent situation just waiting to be said yes to. It's all so big. And not a little scary. Still, as we're parking the car and walking up the drive to her aunt and uncle's, I'm thrilled we're taking this next step.

We're in motion, totally. We both sense the importance of the moment. We're heading to the backyard, where the extended family is barbecuing in July. Allison's from the deep Upper Peninsula, and so her parents made a ten-hour drive to get here. This is a drive I will get to know very well over the next decade.

But just then . . . it feels like her Finnish family comes from Finland itself. I hadn't been close with a Finnish person before Allison. Through her I will get to know an entire culture. They're an incredibly hardy (and hearty), do-it-yourself kind of people. Years later, Allison will fix the electricity in the first house we ever buy. She will open and close the swimming pool herself. She will cut the dog's nails and make furniture out of fallen trees she'll gather from the woods around our house. I will hear her chainsaw blaring outside as I write novels for Del Rey, Penguin Random House. Neighbors and landscaping crews will quickly discover it's Allison they need to talk to if they're talking repairs. Everyone in her family is this way. My instinct is to call someone if I get a flat tire; theirs is to make a tire out of discarded rubber. This will become one of the things I love most about Allison. And maybe it already is, as we reach the gate to the backyard, as a giant brown dog leaps toward us and barks so loud I recoil, even as Allison's father yells for the dog to get down, yells in the booming voice of the pastor he is, a voice that emerges from features as strong as his daughter's.

Yeah, I'm nervous when I meet Allison's family.

And Kenickie. Her strong blond cousin who would climb up onto a roof with no ladder to fix a shingle. He looks to me, then looks to Allison, and reminds everybody here that Allison might need more time being single.

"Already?" he asks her.

Ouch. Not a great start.

But Allison's as tough as her cousin, and she brushes this off. Still, it's been a long time since I "met the family." It's not until I learn her mom is a librarian that I start to feel at ease. The Jack and Cokes help. I feel like I can talk, be myself, even express how I'm feeling about her daughter. Years later, I'll number Allison's parents as two of my close friends. I'll talk books with her mom, sports and politics with her dad. Both big readers. Both unendingly encouraging to me about my own writing.

But that day . . .

A breakthrough comes with Kenickie when he learns I wrote the theme song to *Shameless*. Turns out he loves the show. He asks me to play it for him on the acoustic guitar Allison brings with her everywhere. I play it for him, but in E, the way I originally wrote it, and he's a little drunk and I'm a little drunk and suddenly we're laughing and talking about songs and horror and writing and life on the road. All this under a hot July sky.

And the word *momentum* comes to mind again. How I'd written "The Luck You Got" outside a house party in Athens, Georgia, how I showed it to Mark that night, how he said let's do it, how I was open to our bandmate Berko's complete reworking of the song, raising it four keys, adding more rhythm, turning a small song into a rocker. And Chad's opening lead: one of the best moments in the history of bass guitar.

I'm thinking how that theme song changed the way Allison's family, her cousin at least, saw me. And I'm wondering if Kenickie jives with the spirit of "The Luck You Got" because he, too, exists on a phenomenological plane. Allison's entire family does. They grow their own vegetables, hunt their own meat, fix their own cars, make their own fires, then sit by those fires and look up to the stars so close to Canada. They build their own saunas and, not long after meeting them I will run from one of these saunas, down wooden steps, up the long dock, and leap into a Northern Michigan lake when the thermostat outside tells me it's only forty-eight degrees.

These are Finnish people. And my suburban Jewish mind will be opened a little more every time I hang out with them.

Like the night we watch *The Evil Dead* with Kenickie and Rose.

If ever there's a night I'd call phenomenological, it's the night we watch the movie. Imagine experience itself as vapors. Think individual wisps, a seabed of dark weeds swaying (contentedly or troubled both) with the waves. Imagine experience itself rising, enveloping you, the whole of it an ambush. And because you have eyes only in the front of your head, you can't know every detail of the most memorable elements. Not by sight. Not by sound, smell, taste, or touch. But you can remember, in full, how a thing *feels*.

This is how many of us experience books.

And it's often how we describe them: not the plot or the planning, but the memory of what the book did to us.

It's also the biggest link I've found between writing songs and novels. In the High Strung, our bassist, Chad Stocker, played lead for a long time. But it was and sometimes still is a lead bass. Back in the trio days, I stayed home with Derek, an unconventional rhythm section of drums and guitar, as Chad went off. So, all the traditional pieces were there (rhythm, melody, and so on), but they performed different roles. It was all a lesson for the writing to come:

Find the beat of the story, stick to the beat of the story, for the duration of the rough draft. We can overdub lead lines and harmonies when we rewrite. We can mix and master later. And sometimes you don't need to add a thing. Sometimes, like when Booker T. & the MG's record a song, the basic groove is enough. *Bird Box* was written this way: One beat carried through every scene. You could hold one low note on a synthesizer through all 290 pages, but if you touched a single other key, just one, it would change the entire feel. *Bird Box* didn't need any more than the one beat and the one note. And doing something ridiculous like allowing readers to "see" the creatures on the page would've splintered both these musical elements apart.

With every book I write, there's an invisible drummer sitting behind my office chair. She plays the beat, and I write to *her*. Sometimes she fools me and plays a jazzy thing, 5/4, 11/9, and when I return months later to the rough draft, I have no idea what she was thinking. But I take extra care with those books: Just because you can't remember the beat of the rough draft doesn't mean you won't. There was a reason you wrote it that way the first time around. It's not always a matter of not knowing what you're doing in the rough draft, though many of us joke that it is. Really: With the wild drafts, try to find that wild rhythm again. Let the initial embarrassment wash over you, because if there's one thing people overreact to, it's a thing that embarrasses them. So, let the rough draft tell you what you laid down, and why. And if you can't find it? Well, screw it then. Force a 4/4 on the book and see if that works after all. For me, *Bird Box, Carpenter's Farm, Incidents Around the House* . . . the invisible drummer used a big bass drum for these. She came into the office with marching-band gear. That big-band bass, a harrowing snare shot. Meanwhile, on *Unbury Carol* and *Ghoul n' the Cape,* she showed me every fill she knows.

If you're anything like me, you like all kinds of music.

So why not make it?

All kinds?

All this to say: Once you find that rhythm, you don't need to know the details. You can move by instinct, you can tap your boot. You can *feel* the book, the story, unfolding. You know when it's right to unveil the landmark moment and you know when it's best to keep quiet. But you gotta have that rhythm first. That spine.

The rough draft of a novel can be the gutsiest experience of your life. The odyssey of a lifetime. And it doesn't have to be your first book, the one that gets all this rock 'n' roll. Every time we sit down to write we can tune in. To the phenomenological side.

The experience.

All so we get the most important thing on paper first.

The ghosts, the demons, the dogs: the individual imprint of the writer.

I have rituals. Do you? I think we ought to, the way we're

working with spirit, the spirit we put into a thing. I like to dress up when I write. Cowboy boots. Black pants. A black suit jacket and a button-up shirt. I like the collar buttoned all the way. I treat the rough draft with respect because it's my partner. For the duration. For the dance. Why not follow its lead?

I play records for the both of us, me and the rough draft. And for our drummer too. There's a trashy '80s record player beside my desk. There are shelves of vinyl in the office. I dress up, I put on a record, and I sit down to the draft like I'd sit down to a first date's dinner.

Do you know what you're going to get? I might ask. *Are you ready to order?*

The draft is always ready.

Follow its lead . . .

I've got other rituals. Words I won't use because I don't want them anywhere near the book. I'm not talking about dirty words or dark words: think more like words you wouldn't want someone thinking while reading your book. I'd tell you them, but . . . hey.

I wink, too, at the page when I write a scene I particularly like. I give the page a wink. I send myself editorial emails as if I'm not the writer. I interview myself out in the driveway when taking breaks.

There is no umbrella routine I follow religiously, but each book seems to find its own. *Bird Box* was written between the hours of eight A.M. and noon every day for twenty-six days in October of 2006. I would wake at seven, turn on the coffeepot, start by eight. Around noon (and about 4,300 words) I would stop, go live out the rest of the day. But *Ghoul n' the Cape* was different. It followed its own routine. One thousand words a day. *Incidents Around the House* was about 2,500, mostly around eight P.M. to midnight. And it feels like a novel that could be written only at night.

All this to say: to each book its own. Think: book over author. And to each their own lead. No rules to follow, not even self-imposed. Yet still listening to the book itself, to the where and when of it, to the how-long and how-many-hours too.

What is routine if not stasis? Let's try freehand, typewriter, the computer, and why not dictation? Maybe there's a breakthrough to be had there.

"You could record a book on the 4-track," Allison says. "Then you'd have four times the length of tape."

"And instead of rewriting," I say, "I could just overdub a crash cymbal to cover up a bad line."

We're getting ready to go out. We're upstairs in the house we're renting. I'm wearing the same thing I write in.

Allison is only hours away from watching *The Evil Dead*.

"We should call a car," I say.

I hear a knock then on that inner door. I haven't heard from the man in the fog, the man with the question, for a few days, despite the fact everything I'm doing revolves around *Bird Box*. But a car is a luxury. And if you're wearing a suit, waiting on a beautiful woman, walking the halls of a house, you might start tracing how you got there.

"What does an artist deserve?" I ask.

But I ask nobody. Allison is still upstairs. I'm looking out the front first-floor windows now, my mind wandering. The question slides over me, billowing curtains. I barely examine it.

But still, I know by now it's not going away.

In the end we drive our own car. And on the way I'm thinking about routines and reinvention. And how *Evil Dead 2* is so unbelievably different from the first *Evil Dead*, despite the two starting from the same place. It's a magic trick, what Sam Raimi did there. He reinvented himself while using almost the exact same story elements. Just when he must have been either feeling some pressure to succeed or at least some sense of wanting to outdo what he'd already done. He took a leap between the first two installments and another before the third.

Yet I wonder if there can ever be a bigger leap than the first, the creation of that first . . .

That office we visited . . . they were young men then, trying to sell a movie. *Making* the movie is the biggest leap of all. But just because you find footing upon that first landing, it doesn't mean you have to stay there. In fact, the reason the first leap is the biggest (no leap like it, none as windy) is not because you've leapt up but *out*. You're no longer someone who wants to make a film, *wants* to write a book. Now you are someone who has. You're every bit a writer as someone who's written fifty novels. Because you leapt, because you got your one, your first, and nothing can erase that distance. But the ground you land upon isn't the same ground you started on. New worlds out there, spotted straightaway. New terrain, trees, faces, smells, sounds. New wants too. All a recalibration in the new place because now you know you can do it. There's no longer the question of whether you have it in you, though how could you have known this was never a question to begin with? Still: Landing comes with some responsibility. Do you stay where you landed? Make a cabin, warm your feet by the fire? And why not? There's great pride to be found at the other end of that leap. Get cozy and nobody would blame you one bit. If you wrote your one book as a young person, it's something you'd likely bring up for years, with friends, with lovers, with your family even as your family grows old. And likely they'd speak with pride about the book you wrote, the film you made. They'd visit your comfy cabin, and you'd have sweet coffee to share with them. And as the steam rose pleasantly from those mugs you would not think of what the world might look like if you'd taken a second leap.

A second book. A second work of art.

Or maybe you *would*. Right?

I wonder . . . those who profess satisfaction with making a single work of art . . . do they never look out the cabin window to that second leap? Do they never wonder what terrain is just one leap further away?

Anybody can opt to take that path at any time. Ten, twenty years after that first leap. Or the very next day. You don't even have to look out the cabin window, not at first: You can feel there's *more* inside you. By staying active, staying in writing shape, in idea shape, always open to stories no matter where you look. These leaps become simpler, though not necessarily shorter. I suppose someone could say they get more complex, and I just might pivot on that dime; I just might agree.

"Aren't they up the street from the Blarney Stone?" I ask.

We're driving north on Woodward. Allison has the passenger mirror down, putting her face on.

"Yeah," she says. "But their house will be a Blarney Stone of its own."

I smile. And I think: Imagine who you could become out there. You, with a second leap! Imagine the reinventions. Imagine writing so much you no longer feel like a singular work has to represent you in full. Because the more you work, the more dispersed that spotlight becomes, until you find yourself trying things, new things, for the sake of the leap itself. Like writing nonfiction in a fiction world, decades of novels behind you. Imagine how you might feel out there, down the path, a leap, another path, a leap. Another work of art.

Whom might you meet? Whom might you like? What might you eat? What might you hike? And with all these new sights and sounds, surely new ideas must come. Sides of you that you never imagined.

And I think: There's nothing more revelatory than a new point of view, and there's no quicker way to find one than by doing something you've never done.

A new self-image. Who is this person? And what might they write?

I respect the artist who stays in that first cabin, who invites those they love into their home. I've met many on my way, leaping, still, as I go. So many different cabins at so many different stops along the way. One book, two books, three books, ten. Old, young, women, men. The leaps (and bounds) these people took behind the scenes, where some artists are constantly prepared to leap again, and some have already traveled exactly where they wanted to go.

"I'm real excited for you to see this movie," I say.

"So am I," Allison says.

Oh, the demons you'll see . . .

I think of the Michigan State sweatshirt. I'm excited to point it out when the time comes. But I'll soon see I remembered it wrong. In my memory it was old-school green with solid white lettering. But that's not what the actor wears.

And that's the thing: I'm not an expert on *The Evil Dead*. I wouldn't be able to deliver a speech on its historical significance or recite the credits. But I remember how the movie makes me *feel*.

I'm just a guy, excited to show his girlfriend one of the greatest horror movies ever made.

We drive. We anticipate.

We're in love.

What else matters? Between people, what else?

O art! And the love of it.

That unstoppable roving spotlight.

And the demons and the directors and the directions it reveals.

Too.

COME WHAT MAY, IT'S JUST US ON A BOAT

I KISSED A GUY WHILE STANDING on a pool table at the Blarney Stone one dark and stormy night. We'd been shooting pool for hours and one bet led to another. The place erupted. We were heroes. I remember worrying my cowboy boots might tear the felt fabric on the table. But how long can you worry with sudden shots in each hand, pool sticks clattering to the floor?

A lot of wild party nights in those days. Five, six a week. It was the most broke I've ever been, but a golden stretch of life. Glory be, we had a crew of about fifteen guys and gals, more than a dozen hypnotic personalities, all with unique varieties of instabilities. We painted the town Skittles. A five-year run that became our high school, our college, long after both of those institutions were behind us.

I'm thinking of that crew as Allison and I head north on Woodward. As we pass the Blarney Stone on the left. I'm thinking how I wrote *The Two Drunk Pool Players* and *(PEST)* during that broke, buzzed, happy run. I'd also started writing fictional letters to a friend named only "A" on Facebook. The "A" posts reached some forty thousand words and I absolutely number them now as one of my books. That's the thing: not only are there no rules to what you can write about but no rules to *how you write it* (process), what state you're in, whether you feel good or bad, what medium you use—all.

What constitutes a book? What counts?

Maybe you're a surrealist at heart and dream of three hundred pages of non sequitur language. Maybe you're a cubist who wants to copy and paste passages like Gertrude Stein once did. Books are films or albums or sculptures. Why should we stick to any one style of writing them?

As we're driving, I'm a year away from my first book being published, and I'm already fearing stasis. I won't dismiss a good idea just because I'm hell-bent on change, but I don't want to lean on anything either. It's all gotta touch that nerve. That's it. When the conceit strikes . . . it's gotta light the pyre.

And it doesn't matter *how* we touch that nerve, so long as we achieve ignition. O, horror, O, to find that deeply unsettling place, twice as potent as a surprise leap from a cat or a sudden phone ringing. Stanley Kubrick touched that nerve in *The Shining.* Iain Reid does it with every book. Dathan Auerbach too. It's when you feel you're being subliminally targeted. When the scares are coming off-page. When the experience of *reading* the book haunts you more than any particular scene.

Phenomenological. Again. And a university professor

sitting in front of hundreds of wide-eyed students who adore his theatrics.

One of those students, me. I wrote ideas in a notebook, daily. Rudimentary remarks I believed one day had to become books or songs. Some of them made it. Others were incomprehensible when I read them back. These were the days I started understanding the grandeur of throwing everything against the wall. I started seeing living as a constant flow of ideas—in every interaction, every conversation, every drive to the local store. The individual aisles at Target were packed with ideas. So were the people who worked there. So were the people driving on the same roads to get there. So were the neighborhoods some of those cars turned toward. The streets, the homes, the sky above those homes. The hell-black infinity beyond that sky.

It's the experience, the process, *our* process, not linear historical proof of how it's done! Depth can be dug through subtlety or surprise, loud or soft. We horror writers pride ourselves on truly scaring someone. I sure do. No matter how professional we think we are, no matter how lofty our goals, when you *scare* someone, bottoms up: *you did it*. And for the most part, we all know which scenes of our own reach that peak. But what's the hurry? Why get there right away? And if to unsettle is to succeed (or even to partially succeed), does it matter how that's achieved? I often dream of a novel with no plot, no characters, a roving setting, shifting style. Not a dream but déjà vu. Images, flashes, lightning across the subconscious sky. Could this be maintained for three, four, five hundred pages? And why not . . . a book in which any page the reader opens to is a good place to start. A scary one too.

Phenomenological. The experience.

Allison and I stop at a liquor store on Woodward. Jack and Coke for me, tequila for her. As we enter, I feel like I'm walking like someone who just got a book deal. This is new. It kinda messes me up a little. The book isn't even out yet, but it has already been optioned for film and I know people around town know this. This doesn't make me famous. But whether you're humble or not, grateful or not, getting a book deal changes things. After writing for nearly twenty years without one, it adds a nice spring to your step, something you can turn to when you're feeling weird. Does it solve things? Well, some. It can help. A little bit. And a little bit is something.

The difference between satisfaction and total freak-out is often that little bit.

I start thinking about how safe or unsafe it is to find identity through success. But then I ask myself to explain success. Then I'm rolling my eyes at myself, thinking, Of *course* you're asking to define success the moment after thinking you found a little. Not for doubting it, but because it's been ingrained in most people to *not* feel comfortable defining success.

I hear that inner question again. And the word.

Deserve . . .

This time it doesn't come quite as vague. The faceless

man in the overcoat standing in the fog might've slipped a piece of paper under that inner door. It smells damp.

"Ice," I tell Allison. "There's nothing worse than running out of ice. One winter my friend Alex and I used the ice from his roof in our drinks."

"I don't think you're supposed to do that."

"We didn't think so either."

It's bright in the liquor store. Always is. While Allison gets the tequila and ice, I'm thinking of what I've come to call the Four V's:

Vindication.

Victory.

Validation.

Vengeance.

I won't let the Four V's anywhere near me or my writing. I know this is intrinsically tied to my idea of identity and success, both. A lot to think on here.

The Four V's . . .

I don't want to feel any of these things at any time in connection with my writing. If a handful of the thousands of people I've met over the course of my life doubted I would amount to anything? Okay. Great. A few people didn't believe I'd ever be published? That's just fine. Cool. We're talking percentages here, numbers. I care so little about this, I feel strange even mentioning it here. One or two people don't believe in you? Believe you me, there were nights I spoke of books, books I was writing, and felt the sympathetic gazes of those within earshot. I'm thinking of a college girlfriend's mom who looked mortified when I answered her question of what I wanted to do with my life by telling her I already was doing it.

I'm thinking of a friend who told me I needed a plan B.

I'm thinking of the people who asked why I'd write a second novel (*Goblin*) without having yet sold the first (*Wendy*).

I'm thinking of the inescapable thrust of needing to write more, of wanting to write more, of wanting the tower of rough drafts to grow taller than me. Now, today, this pile of pages exists. And as I grab the bottle of Jack from the shelf in the Woodward liquor store, I feel no V's toward those people from my past whatsoever.

The book deal is no Victory.

A good review does not Validate.

An award is not Vindication.

Sales are not Vengeance.

I feel (I demand) a militant optimism in their stead. A persistent swatting-away of these V's.

Can I really expect the non-artist to understand that the victory is not in sales but in writing the book itself? Can someone who doesn't write be expected to understand that the words *THE END* and not *on the dotted line* are the finish line?

"We're gonna end up spending the night, aren't we?" Allison says.

"Yeah."

Because we don't drive on nights we drink.

We step up to the counter, and I'm still focused on the V's and this new identity as a man with a book deal who is now buying a bottle of whiskey. I can't pretend there isn't a change in me. A relief. And some of that is money but most of it is the fact that a vaguely outlined fantasy of mine has come true. Sooner rather than later, *Bird Box* will be a book on a bookstore shelf. Maybe even shelved next to Richard Matheson.

"Maybe we should bring something for them," Allison says. Though we both imagine since it's their house they'll have drinks of their own.

"Beer?" I ask. "Kenickie seems like a beer guy."

Yoopers. They like beer.

"I was thinking wine," Allison says. "For Rose."

I actually met Rose, Kenickie's girlfriend, before I met Allison. She worked in a Barnes & Noble near a house where I slept on a mattress in a hall. She and a guy named Guppy guided me through the new releases in the horror section. I cherished the hell out of those moments. I learned from them. But this would be my first time hanging with Rose outside the store. The fact she's been dating Allison's cousin for years was enough to blow my mind.

And the fact we're going to hang out with a bookseller is on my mind.

Those aisles . . . those shelves . . .

Allison goes to get the wine.

One day people will ask if seeing Sandra Bullock play Malorie is the most surreal moment of my life. Well, yes.

The Audrey Hepburn of our generation, playing one of my favorite characters to write. I cried when Allison and I saw her on the screen at Netflix headquarters in Los Angeles. We were in a screening room called the Upsidedown, and there were no previews, no ads. There was popcorn. And then there's Sandra Bullock, asking Boy and Girl if they "understand" the rules she's laying down, and I was brought back to writing that scene at the giant oak desk in the third-floor ballroom of the place I rented in 2006. So, yes. But also . . .

Not even close.

Can anything top the surrealism of a fantasy becoming reality? How many faux interviews did I conduct with myself over the years, asking questions I wanted so badly to one day answer? How many arguments did I have with not-yet-existent editors, managers, agents, thinking (wrongly) that debates must be part of a life of letters? And the books themselves, imagined on the shelves in whatever house I lived in, and every bookstore I entered . . .

How can anything be more surreal than witnessing these vague reveries become substantial reality as the black-and-white sketch of a writer's life was colored in, all in real time?

I hadn't imagined Sandra Bullock (or anybody) playing Malorie. Malorie was only Malorie—raven-haired, a white tank top, pregnant in a house loaded with philosophical archetypes. I relate to Malorie more than any other character I've written. In some ways the housemates are all points of view, potential reactions to a world gone mad. She roots for the optimist (Tom) while still listening to the admonishments of the pessimist (Don). Don was right, after all, when he said they shouldn't let Gary in. Yet, even so, did pessimism triumph? No. Malorie makes sure of that. Just as I, and a lot of us, try to do in our daily lives. Optimism must at least have a seat at the table.

"I got a bottle of red," Allison says. "Rosé felt too much like a pun."

We pay. We leave. We head south now on Woodward, back toward the Blarney Stone. We turn right.

"The white one there," Allison says.

We pass their house, and I slow to park at the curb. Royal Oak is a suburb of Detroit. Back in high school it was hip to the point of being intimidating. My mom took me into Noir Leather without telling me what they sold and she just kinda watched me discover an alternative world. I still see it like she intentionally opened a door to the idea that life can be more than good grades and whatever profession might follow. I think she saw a young man following a path a little too strictly back then. The books in that store had names I couldn't repeat at school. I was captain of the cross-country team and I wanted to take everyone I knew to Royal Oak, where the stores weren't just for adults but also for outlaws. The city is a few miles up Woodward from Ferndale, that of the *Evil Dead* office and the public bathroom, of course. Kenickie and Rose lived in a very cool part of town. The houses are smaller in

Ferndale and most of Royal Oak, but nobody who lives there is thinking much of staying home. These are vibrant areas, suburban vivid. I'm feeling the energy of the city as I turn off the car, as we get out and carry the bottles to the front door.

We don't have to knock. The inner door is open and through the glass of the outer door I see Rose and a Chihuahua. Rose sees us, lowers her glasses to make sure, and lights up with a smile. When she opens the door, we're hit with what feels like an entire block's worth of marijuana.

This is gonna be a night.

"You guys!" Rose says. "I'm so fuckin' excited. *The Evil Dead!* Oh, and this is Clip."

I lived with a Chihuahua back when I wrote *Bird Box.* Clip seems nicer than that one.

"It's good to see you out of the bookstore," I say.

"Yes! Here we are in the real world."

"Well . . ."

"Right. I mean, how *real* am I talking, here?" Then: "Have you seen the remake yet?"

"No," I say. "It just came out?"

"Yeah! And you," she says to Allison. "You haven't seen any of this?"

A loud crash from the kitchen. The sound of a dish tossed onto other dishes. And a figure in the kitchen doorway.

For a second, I catch a frown, then Kenickie realizes we're here.

In a novel I might've asked, *Did we come at a bad time?*

But he smiles, too, his blond hair an immediate reminder he's Allison's cousin.

"Dudes!" he says. "Why'd you bring booze? We got booze!"

Then everybody's talking at once. Kenickie is listing off the drinks they have, Allison is talking about the wine we brought, I'm saying hey it's better to be sure of these things, and Rose is thanking us for the bag of extra ice.

"This movie is gonna blow your mind," Kenickie tells Allison. "It's the most badass horror movie ever made. The *Godfather* of horror. I should talk to your folks about not having showed you before."

"Well, Dad did take me to see *Se7en* when I was seven."

"*Wow*," Rose says. "That's actually really fucked-up."

Kenickie smiles like a wicked kid. He'll do this a lot tonight. "That's the Mike I love."

The girls talk about little Clip by the front door as I follow Kenickie to the kitchen and I'm thinking of how he said *The Evil Dead* is the *Godfather* of horror. Barometers. And can you imagine writing a novel that becomes a barometer?

"Jack and Coke? Really?" Kenickie asks. "Don't you have a movie deal? I've got better stuff."

"What do you have?"

"Let me see . . ."

"I've been drinking this since I was seventeen," I say. "Jack and Coke never turns on me."

"It's the Coke."

"Likely."

He hands me a glass. Calls out to Allison. "Hey, Al, you're not drinking this high school shit, right?"

"Right," Allison says.

Then she and Rose and Clip are at the kitchen door. I smile at Allison. We were in different rooms for one fuckin' minute and it feels good to see her again.

Kenickie opens the freezer. He's got a joint in his mouth now. Bites it like a strand of wheat.

"I used to live with a Chihuahua," I tell Rose. "Loved that dog. But it bit me in my sleep. On my face. I woke up to being bit on the face."

"Yeah well, Clip isn't staying," Kenickie says.

I catch a dark look pass between him and Rose. That's the second scowl I've seen since we arrived. The scene is a little off-beat. *Is this a good time?*

"We're just fostering Clip," Rose says.

Drinks are being poured. Our voices are already animated. There's classic horror to be watched. Soon, and in the dark.

"Congrats on your book deal," Rose says.

"Thank you," I say. "It's all been amazing. I meet Allison and then a few months later I get a book deal. It's . . . a lot of good stuff at once."

"That is a lot!" she says. "And man, I remember you coming into B&N asking about the horror section, why we didn't have one. Me and Guppy would help you find good stuff anyway."

"Yes," I say. "I love that guy."

Her face changes. A sympathetic frown. I worry what she's gonna say next.

"Actually, he didn't like you," she says.

"Rose," Kenickie says. "What the fuck?"

But Rose ignores this. "When I told him about your book deal, he rolled his eyes."

"Really?" I say. "What does that mean?"

"It's a bummer thing to say is what it is," Kenickie says.

I have bright memories of Guppy walking me down aisles, the two of us smiling about Lovecraft, Matheson, more. I can see him in complete detail, from his hair to his glasses, the look in his eye, his smile. I spent hours of my life listening to him recommend horror novels.

"Welp, that sucks," Allison says.

"Sorry," Rose says. "But you said you love him, and I didn't think you should be in the dark on that."

"No, it's okay," I say. "I mean . . . I guess that's how it is. But . . . shit."

Another offbeat. We've been here not even five minutes.

"Who gives a fuck?" Kenickie says. "Here."

He hands me a drink. Has one for himself.

"Cheers, dude," he says. "To *The Evil Dead*."

We all toast.

Kenickie is talking about seeing *The Evil Dead* at a

drive-in years ago, but I haven't quite shaken that Guppy news. It's my first instance of someone who isn't glad to hear I got a book deal. It won't be the last.

I hear the knocking on the inner door. The faceless man in the fog is waiting for an answer. *What does an artist deserve?* I guess it's clear Guppy didn't think I deserved a book deal. This, of course, is without him having read *Bird Box*. My memory of the two of us walking the aisles is changed now: I see myself as some wide-eyed Pollyanna, charged up, so excited to discover new (to me) scary stories. I'd felt a bond with him. Yet, all that time . . .

Or was it something that happened since those days? He was a writer himself. I think of the Four V's. I shove away any sense of Vindication here.

But there's a small warring of emotions within me. Small, but feisty. Nobody likes to be disliked, and nobody expects everybody to like them, but this feels especially sudden. The fact Rose told me at all, and this early in the night.

I was a runner in high school, I wore Detroit Pistons shirts and listened to the doo-wop music Dad played me and my brothers. I didn't know what I liked back then. I liked it all. From metal to folk, harmony groups to New Age pan flute music. Once the band (the High Strung) started in earnest, I started worrying we were too hippie for the rockers and too rock for the hippies. I started to feel like a "tweener," something I'd experience years later after publishing some dozen novels, sensing from the audience a righteous rooting for the indie authors, yet an undying allegiance to the all-time bestsellers. Again, I would find myself . . . between. Yet, I found purgatory (imagined or otherwise) pleasant enough. And this lack of a "brand" will eventually be evident on my book covers, as there will be no uniformity to the style, no signature font for my name. I'll be asked in dozens of interviews if I intentionally set out to write books that are nothing like the ones before them, and while I will take pride in the question (the answer is no), I'll also worry, a little, because a lot of people like a brand. They like a brand because they can pledge their allegiance to whatever that definitive brand is. How do you pledge allegiance to a man who maybe doesn't like "horror" but is asking after Matheson, Rollo, and the Satanic Bible?

But also, hey . . . right now? Whatever. Let's drink.

"You've never seen *The Evil Dead*?" Kenickie asks me. Music is playing in the living room. Allison is talking to Rose about fostering a dog. Allison wants a dog. She's brought up getting a Weimaraner. I've liked those dogs from afar forever but when I looked them up online, I found a list of warnings. Turns out they're neurotic, superintelligent Velcro dogs. Years later, when, for whatever reason, our Weimaraner Valo doesn't follow me around the house, I'll be calling out for her, asking her to please come bother me. We'll love her and Tuli (a Vizsla) like they're our children. The dogs of our lives.

"Oh, I sure have," I say.

When Kenickie smiles, his eyes vanish in squints. But I can sense something is amiss with him and Rose.

It's got me thinking of arcs. In ourselves. In relationships.

Allison and I are just starting out. Where are Kenickie and Rose?

While I haven't got a book published yet by the night we watch *The Evil Dead,* I have written more than a dozen novels and probably the same number of albums. The High Strung wrote songs during sound checks; I wrote novels in the passenger seat of our touring van. Four of my first eight were written freehand. I remember the boys going to check out a city embedded in the side of a mountain in New Mexico while I stayed in a hotel bar, writing. I missed some key moments out on the road. Some night in Tombstone. Another at Crater Lake, Oregon.

I worry sometimes that I'm missing too many cities in the sides of mountains. But I remind myself that in order to finish a work of art, sometimes you gotta say no to something else.

No rules for writing, but maybe there's some guilt when I don't.

Once you begin a book, work on it every day until it's done.

There's a routine in that, and there's also not. "Working on it" could mean a page. Half a page. It could mean a forty-page eruption. While Kenickie talks about the very office building Allison and I christened, I'm thinking of the arc of the artist. I'm thinking of the *Evil Dead* guys and where they were on their own arc when they made their first movie. While (like I said) I'm not an expert on the films, I do know some things. They filmed all sorts of weird shit with smaller cameras before they made that first classic feature. Did they already feel like old men by the time they made part 2? Like how the Beatles spoke of themselves as feeling old at twenty-seven?

Here's what haunts me:

How close we all are to writing a classic. If you're short on skill? Maybe the narrator should be too. If you tend to overwrite? Lean into that. Or force yourself into the opposite. Or don't. All of which is to say: We're one decision away from a masterpiece. At all times. Rather than grieve your self-doubt, maybe the next book should expose your self-doubt—intentionally. And maybe the older we get, the easier it is to admit, no, *underscore* our shortcomings. Or maybe it's harder?

The writer, as we already know, is ageless.

People consider Hemingway's last book his best. *The Old Man and the Sea* might've been a slim novel, but it's as potent as anything he ever dreamed of doing. But the argument for "ageless" has less to do with *when* someone does their best work and more to do with consistently working in the first place. Again, imagine a non-artist. Your grandfather, let's say. And your grandfather worked for General Motors here in Michigan. And every time you went to Grandfather's house, you ate the butterscotch

candies he and Grandmother had out in a dish. You expected the refreshingly tasteless jokes. You expected the
good times. You expected the inquiries into your own life;
your grandparents seemed more interested than most in
your plan. Then, one night, maybe when you were still a
tween, someone brought up that Grandfather wrote a
book. You were amazed at this. You'd recently discovered
good books yourself. You were just starting to wonder if
you might not try your hand at one. You were even considering telling him about this feeling you have, when you
read books, *the call of the covers.* How differently do you
look at your grandfather when you learn he wrote a book?
How much more color and depth does this add to your
understanding of him? Do you consider him smarter?
Cooler? Does it almost frighten you, the potentialities in
this news? Does it imply doors and hallways in everyone
you meet? Surprise corridors, even in those you call family,
even in those you know and love? And now imagine you
learned he *just* wrote it. Only days before you found out.
Grandpa's been writing . . . a book? And he finished it?
What would this tell you about him? And how would you
describe your grandfather for the decades to follow?

As a man who worked for General Motors and liked
dirty jokes?

Or as a man who wrote a book, a book you would no
doubt read, a man who fulfilled an uncharacteristic goal,
making it therefore . . . entirely characteristic?

I imagine there wouldn't be a single friend of yours who

didn't know the name of your grandfather's book. Some of them might've read it. A lot of them. And who knows? Maybe, just maybe, Grandpa's book was *good*.

Arcs . . . and where we're at on them . . .

"Josh, you wanna step outside?" Kenickie asks. He's holding the joint between two fingers now. I haven't decided if I wanna smoke grass or not. I usually don't. It can turn me inward. At the same time, it's already getting harder to say no, tonight, in this place that smells like it's made of the stuff. Drink in hand, Allison near, a classic movie to watch.

"Sure," I say.

But when we step out to the backyard, I don't take a hit. I talk with him while he does. We're standing next to a pair of big garbage cans. He's telling me about roofing houses, it's one of many things he does. He talks about it the way I talk about books.

"We've got guys on the team who hate doing it," he says. "They *say* they hate roofing, but they like when the roofing is done. So why do it? Way I see it, we're outside, under the sun. We're at a different job site all the time. The money's all right too. I live here, I've got a roof of my own. Got a drink. Got a joint. Right? What the fuck more could you want?"

"Okay, fine, I'll take a hit," I say.

"There you go."

He hands it over. I pinch it, take the tiniest hit. I've been ambushed by creepers before.

"Figured a guy like you would be smoking grass all the time," he says. "In a band, writing scary shit. If I was writing scary shit, I'd get super high and put it all in the book."

This suddenly sounds like the best philosophy for writing horror I've ever heard. Kenickie will hit me with dozens of nuggets like this throughout the night.

"Well, the way you put it . . ." I say. Then I cough and I'm worried I took more than the tiniest bit. I know enough about grass to know what the cough means.

"You're gonna get high now," he says.

I cough for what feels like twenty minutes.

"So, I've tried it once," I tell him finally. "I got drunk and high for one book. Wrote it freehand and figured, why not one, one book, kinda fucked-up?"

"Hell yeah, man. If it doesn't mess with you."

"Well, that's kinda it. I'd just stare at a sentence forever, as if it might rewrite itself."

"Isn't that what all writing is?"

See? All night, this guy.

"In a way it is," I say. "But that sounds more romantic than how it goes."

"I bet."

He offers me another hit, but I pass. It feels good being out here, under a Michigan sky.

"Rose and me," he says. "Things are a little fucked-up."

"Ah."

"Yeah, you can tell."

"I guess so."

"She's on me about everything. I'm on her about everything. I don't know." He looks past me, out toward the dark alley that runs behind their house. "It's good to see you guys, though. Good to have you here." Then, "Maybe *The Evil Dead* will make everything right."

The optimist in me likes the way he says it. And maybe it will. And maybe, for some, that's the point of a movie, a book, art. Or of roofing, too, or any project that requires all of you, body and mind.

Years before this night, the High Strung played a show at the Empty Bottle in Chicago. The poet Thax Douglas asked if he could read a poem before our set. This was/is a badge of honor in Chicago. Thax reads as the opening act for bands he likes. After we played, he and I were standing offstage watching the headliner. I told him I was working on a book. I don't remember which one. I told him I had a fantasy of writing "the great optimist horror novel." I didn't know what this meant exactly. It didn't mean a story that ends on a high note, I knew that much. Had I seen all the David Lynch I'd see years later, I might've given him the example of Agent Dale Cooper in the town of Twin Peaks. An optimist in hell. In the Black Lodge too. But Thax's response took care of this: "Isn't the act of writing in and of itself optimistic?"

At first I thought he meant a writer must imagine a reader if they are writing. They must think someone will read what they write. But I had it wrong. He meant there's *meaning* in the act of writing. Of *doing*. And the fact we do it at all, the fact we do anything at all, is optimistic. Because it implies anything we do means something at all.

"One more hit?" Kenickie asks. If I'd smoked as much as he did on this short trip to the garbage cans, I'd be unable to climb the few steps back into the house. I feel droplets of rain. We both hold out our hands and look up.

"I'm so glad it's about to storm while we watch this movie," I say.

"Fuck yes."

He puts the joint out on his barbecue grill and we head back inside.

The rain comes harder just as we enter.

"Ooh!" Rose says. Clip is trembling from the sound of the downpour against the roof. I think of Kenickie on a roof, wanting to do good work.

"Did you smoke grass?" Allison asks.

"A little one," I say.

"But he coughed," Kenickie says. "So he's high."

Am I? I can't tell. This whole house feels high. The rain sounds like plucks of violin strings. The early inklings of a horror-movie soundtrack.

I go to the counter to refill my Jack and Coke. Already. And we haven't started the movie yet. I fix the drink, but I don't stir it. That's the key to Jack and Cokes. Eyeball the right combination and leave it be. When I exit the kitchen, Allison and Kenickie are on the couch and Rose is in an easy chair with Clip in her lap. They're facing a huge black screen I hadn't noticed when we walked in.

"Oh, we're doing it," I say.

"We're absolutely doing it," Rose says. "Right now."

Kenickie turns on the TV and he's flipping through screens and Rose is telling him how to do it, what to do. They bicker about it. Shoot a few barbs. I don't know anything about TVs and DVDs, and I turn to Allison. She's smiling and it feels like we're alone on a gently rocking boat. Not that the world is turning, but that we are out to sea, and we've been out to sea since we met. I wonder if that's a hallmark of love. The two of you can be anywhere, but when you look at each other, it's just you two, alone on the adventure. It's something I'll come to need, in the years to follow, as horror events become a regular part of my life. From conventions to readings to book launches. Even movie premieres and a red carpet with Sandra Bullock. Even when we were invited on the *Bird Box* set, even there as I met Sandra Bullock for the first time, she in full Malorie wardrobe and makeup, me wearing what I'll come to call the Uniform (a black suitcoat, button-up shirt with black buttons, cowboy boots, hat), with the set lights above us and around us, with the rest of the cast and crew in the deep shadows outside the reach of those lights:

Even then I will be introducing Sandra Bullock to Allison Laakko. Asking Allison to step forth from those shadows. And even then, faced with the celebrity of a generation, I will look to Allison and I will think: *It's just us. On a boat. The two of us on this boat.*

I will cancel two events she can't attend. I will fret about readings without her presence. I will lean on her to make props for the book launches, to dress up as the characters from the novels, with costumes and masks she will make herself. I will play live music as she narrates the part of Malorie the night *Bird Box* is released. She will stand in front of a room full of blindfolded friends and family, in Ferndale, Michigan, black and white balloons tied to each folding chair in the bar. The great Detroit musician/photographer Brian Rozman will capture this moment in a photo that will one day hang in the first house we ever buy. And on the very day I write these words you now read, I will be thinking of how Allison and I and our theatrical troupe, Wow Town, can present *Watching Evil Dead* in a theater.

It will be the fourteenth book I've published. I'll have twenty-six more, waiting in the wings, in crates in my office, as, even after securing a book deal, I won't change the two-books-per-year average I had going before I met Kristin Nelson, before *Bird Box* got picked up.

"If you write fifty books in your life, it's still rarer than a birthday," I say. "Hopefully."

"Told you he was high," Kenickie says. "Love it."

"God willing, we live that long and longer," I go on. "Even fifty books . . . rarer than New Year's Eve."

And with the unwrapping of each novel, we will celebrate. And the feeling upon finishing will be like no other I'll ever know.

But first, before I fill two crates' worth of novels, and as

I wait for my first to be published in a year, we have a movie to watch here.

"Took you long enough," Rose says to Kenickie.

"Why didn't you set it up then?" he asks.

Edges in their voices. Rose smiles my way. It strikes me that whatever they're going through, they once had experienced what Allison and I are experiencing now.

New love.

And I think of books. And the love for them. And how it still feels new to me.

"All right," Kenickie says.

A crash of thunder outside and all four of us laugh. Because it's thundering. And we're about to hit Play on a horror movie.

"Get ready, Al," Kenickie says. "This one is gonna take you places."

He hits Play.

I grab Allison's hand. She grips mine.

And with all these thoughts and backdrops, these questions and affections, these anticipations, wants, and fears . . .

. . . the movie starts.

The Evil Dead begins.

CHERYL, CHERYL, CHERYL

Jesus. The title card alone. And the opening shots low to the water. The wind, the cackles.

What did people think of this back in the day? What possibilities did this immediately unlock in other filmmakers?

I may not be an expert, but I know enough about *The Evil Dead* to know Sam Raimi and company caught lightning. Sam Raimi's style is easy to pick out today; I can't imagine how fresh it felt back then. And to have witnessed the start of this legend's arc . . .

As we watch, I think: Everyone understands it's the *unknown* that scares us most. What's around the corner, what's going to happen to me and who's going to do it? But now let's imagine pulling up to a drive-in. You know nothing about the movie except maybe it's supposed to be scary. You've seen a thousand scary movies, and most of them didn't scare you and so you're laughing, you're hanging with friends, a date, there's some booze in the flask, joints in the glove compartment. You're still thinking of your daily life, the life you live and have always known, a life that does not yet include *The Evil Dead:* The movie has yet to change you. But it's about to. From the title card, the low shots of the water and the fallen leaves, intercut with the carload of five friends, the girl singing up front. The movie has hit the ground running, there is no buildup here; we've begun. It feels different, the camera is moving like we haven't seen a camera move before. We do not *know* this movie yet. The actors have faces we have not seen. For us: This is *all* unknown. We know nothing! And we ask ourselves . . .

Who *made* this?

And do we trust them? This . . . unknown person? Who produced this? And are they dangerous enough to cross a line we've never crossed before? Are we about to experience, see, feel things we've never felt?

How scary is this going to get?

The unknown can extend from the story to the story-*teller.* And that can become the most powerful scare.

Who *made* this? Whose hands are we in?

Man, these early edits, the red truck barreling, the yellow car rolling along, those dolly (?) shots across land and water. And Ash's first words. And Ash's name too. I wonder if people in 1981 had heard the name used for a man since *Gone with the Wind.* Maybe Sam Raimi named him Ash to tie him to a classic, as he was probably the only human being alive who understood he was making one himself.

"This is already cool," Allison says.

"Yes!" Rose says.

These freakin' edits, so wild. Still fresh, now, to all of us. What then, back then?

I think of foreign horror films, and how often it's the editing that scares us. Movies that don't follow the Western arcs are naturally less-known to Westerners. Or have been for a long time. If the movie you're watching doesn't follow the trajectory, the rhythm you know . . . how can you be sure when it's safe? What to do . . . if you can't even trust your own horror-loving instincts.

Phenomenological. Get rid of the traditional details.

Think: *experience.*

Spirit over strategy.

Feel over fashion.

All these roads lead to the unknown.

This is, of course, an argument for writing the story you've always worried was too weird. The one you've never seen before.

And no genre welcomes a newcomer quite like horror.

"What gives it this look?" I ask the room. "Is it the film stock? The age of the film?"

"Their outfits," Rose says.

"It's not their outfits," Kenickie says.

"You can see they're dressed of the times," Rose says. "So we feel transported to an earlier age. It actually is an earlier age. This is the past."

"All movies are the past," Kenickie says.

And did a demon spirit take the wheel just then? Was it trying to keep the young people away? To kill them? But doesn't it want them to come, to read the book, to summon them?

Don't the spirits want to be summoned?

Or maybe they don't. Hadn't thought of that before. And this, my first book idea since we started the movie. I like it, maybe: a spirit, angry for being summoned. Wants to be left alone.

Forgot about the characters getting stuck on the bridge.

And now . . . here they are. The first shot of the cabin. And was this the first of the "cabin" movies? So many since.

It strikes me how a simple thing can become iconic. This exact cabin wouldn't have made you feel uneasy at all if you'd found it yourself in the woods of Tennessee . . . *if* you hadn't seen so many scary movies.

"That rhythmic thudding is great," Allison says. "It's like having music without music."

She's already into this. This is great. Kenickie and Rose are still debating what ages a film.

I like the thudding too. The swinging porch chair, knocking against the cabin door.

"This movie's the template," Kenickie says.

And what's a template and how original does something have to be to qualify for that? What was the template for *The Evil Dead*? There's a look to this movie that nobody had seen before. It's not just the lighting. And while Sam

Raimi may be one or two movies away from cementing his signature style, the look is already there. Seven minutes in and we're already watching shots of Cheryl from behind the pendulum of the grandfather clock. Then, an edit for each chime. This is energy, this is rhythm, this isn't waiting for a story to present itself, this isn't setting the stage. The vibe, the spirit . . . it's all immediately present. You get the feeling Sam Raimi was thinking, *If we're going to roll the camera, why not shoot something extraordinary?* Every single time they called action.

Kenickie lights up another joint.

"Is this their first?" Rose asks.

"Of course it's their first," he says. "That's the whole point. It's the first *Evil Dead*."

"I know that, Kenickie. But their first movie?"

"Why are you saying my name?"

"What do you mean?"

"You only say my name when you're bothered."

"I wasn't bothered. Not a few seconds ago, I wasn't." Then: "Kenickie."

"Of course it's their first. This is the first one. The second is the one with the hand."

"That's not what I'm asking."

"It's their first, yeah," I say. And I'm thinking it's interesting we're saying *their* and not *his,* because, despite how successful Sam Raimi will become, this feels like a team effort. This feels like a group of people went to a cabin in the woods and had the time of their lives.

"Exactly," Kenickie says. "Their first. *The* first. *Evil Dead.*"

The veins in Cheryl's hand when she can't stop drawing the book! The violins! The rattling of the cellar door!

"Does anyone know what lenses they used for this?" I ask. Because it's impossible to watch without wanting to shoot something too. The look. It's all I can think about. The look.

"No idea," Kenickie says. "But it's cool as shit."

And oh man, the first time the cellar door swings open. And the friends all looking down into the dark.

Kenickie hands me the joint. My eyes are glued to the screen. I take it. And why not? This movie is making me want to say yes.

To a lot of things: *yes.*

I'm thinking of firsts. First book. First finished book. I'd been trying for ten years. Failed four times. And by failed I mean did not finish. My entire criterion for successfully writing a novel is finishing the novel. That's it. That's all. It's not an easy thing to explain to someone who hasn't written one. Because what most people do is compare their blank pages to the finished books that inspired them. They're not thinking of the twelve drafts their favorite book went through. The danger here, of course, is that no first draft is going to be close to the tenth. Recently the High Strung wrapped an album we're all crazy about. *Address Unknown.* We want to do something just as good for the next one. But we gotta be smart: Our starting point for the next album can't be the mixed and mastered album we just finished. We need to start the new album the same way we started the one we want to emulate. In other words, Mark and I need to send each other partially finished VM's with half-written verses and la-la lyrics. We gotta start from the same blank slate if we wanna reach a similar finish. Unfortunately, there's some faith involved. It's unlikely any of us are going to get our hands on the rough drafts of the books that inspire us. We're never going to see those books in the same state as our own. And so what is good or bad in our first drafts, and what are we comparing ourselves to, if all we have is the finished works of the greats?

"Don't go down there," Allison says.

I love it. Allison is getting scared.

Now, normally, Allison is brave. Jump-off-a-mountain-in-Brazil brave. Wants-to-swim-with-sharks brave. But put her in front of a movie she doesn't know the ending of? In the years that follow this night of watching *The Evil Dead*, I will witness Allison reach for her phone five hundred times to google how a movie ends.

Meanwhile, I don't remember everything that happens here myself.

Hey, Scotty, you find anything?

I have a vague memory that the man who played Scotty was a teacher at the high school I went to. Is this true? He used a stage name in the movie? If so, why? Did he think it was silly, embarrassing? Was this too much to reconcile with a professional career? There are only five actors in this movie. Did one of them worry it might ruin his teaching-career prospects, being in one of the biggest movies of all time?

"Jesus," Allison says. "I'm sweating."

There's a *clunk* sound in the basement. Ash is down there, looking for Scotty.

Kenickie hands me the joint again, but I pass it to Rose. Eyes on the movie.

So many close-ups. So much camera movement. The sound design. That signature treble of the early '80s. Think: dress shoes on concrete, car doors closing.

The fake lightning! The black cloud spreading across the moon!

At times, this movie feels like a genius child's art project. Shown to the class.

"Uh-oh," Kenickie says.

Because Ash is playing the tape now.

Rose coughs from hitting the joint, and Clip adjusts in her lap.

The more I watch, the more I think it is the lighting after all. Something cartoonish here. You can see this exact lighting in Raimi's later movies like *The Quick and the Dead*. Even *Spider-Man*.

"Here they come," Rose says. She coughs again. She's talking about the demons.

I'm feeling it now. Feeling high. Second drink is almost gone too. Allison sips her tequila.

Ash says, *Why don't we stay up for a while and listen to the storm?*

We all cheer for this line. For the storm clacking against Rose and Kenickie's house too.

Been watching this fuckin' movie less than twenty minutes and we're cheering.

And how about this incredible necklace-exchange scene with the close-up of Ash's and Linda's eyes?

I reach over and take Allison's hand again.

Young love. Years later I will understand the meaning of real love, aged love, a decade deep with this woman. But the night we watch *The Evil Dead* together for the first time, our love is as young as Ash and Linda's.

Can you write a book that feels like this movie? Or an album? I don't mean a book about this movie or an album that quotes it. How would you write a novel that *feels* the way this movie feels?

Rose spills her drink on her lap. Clip leaps out of the way.

"Come on, Rose," Kenickie says. He sounds higher than I am. Drunker too.

"It's not like I meant it," Rose says. "You think someone means it when they spill a drink? That's why it's called an *accident*, dickhead."

I laugh.

"Really?" Kenickie says. " 'Dickhead'? In front of friends and family?"

While their bickering grows into more of a fight, we're

still watching the movie. We can't *not* watch it. Still, I silently acknowledge I had no idea these two were at this place in their relationship. At no time on the drive over did Allison and I prep ourselves for "what might happen." And while I sensed something was up when we arrived, now it's center stage. Couple this with what Rose told me about the bookseller who didn't like me for who knows what reason, and there's some darkness in the air. Not to mention the fact we're watching five innocent people discovering the Necronomicon. I'm starting to sense similarities between the movie and the little scene the four of us make. Because I know the movie, I know Ash will have to do battle with his friends as they're possessed by demons summoned from the book. And while I won't be battling any physical demons tonight, some metaphorical ones are in the house.

Here we sit, Allison and I, in the throes of young love. Faced with, tonight, a mirror of sorts: the end of love, love's end. It's like a whole potential romantic arc is in this house with us. Wasn't there a day when Kenickie and Rose felt similar to how Allison and I do now? And no matter how long ago that day was, don't they feel like it was only yesterday? I squeeze Allison's hand, not just to tell her I love her but to hold on to this thing we've found. And I know the night is young, but so are we. And so are Kenickie and Rose.

But you see? When we talk about what age a person is, what are we referring to? The years one has spent on this planet? Or the passions within those people? How old is your love of reading? How old your love of horror? How old your love of *The Evil Dead*? Where on your character arc are you? Because as we sit in the living room, as the little dog trembles from the thunder outside, the thunder on the screen, and the growing storm of rising voices, I'm thinking of success. Relationship success. And what success means.

And how, for me, it's clear it has something to do with maintaining our relationships with our passions. How much fuel is there in the tank? People change, people grow apart. Is success (in writing) selling a lot of books or is it maintaining the love for writing? Because chances are, any love lost for the medium will not come from within. Not by . . . choice. Years from this night I will have endured dozens of days that might try one's passion. Whether that's from self-doubt, a project underperforming, not getting the idea right on paper, not relating to what is popular, wishing people spoke more about ideas and less about branding, worrying I don't fit into a particular subset of the genre . . . And it will be up to me to maintain my love for the actual writing itself, no matter how loud these surprises get.

Think: When you first set out down the path of writing, what propelled you? What motivated? I fear linear motivation. Sales = success. Reviews = success. Engagement = success. Never mind how gross these types of goals likely make you feel, the real horror is how quickly one can believe they've *failed*. For me, the only failure is not finishing a story that's been started. In a lifetime of writing, it's the only true disappointment I've ever felt.

Here, now, I feel a sudden flash of worry. I didn't hear the faceless man in the fog knocking this time. The word *deserve* has come like an ambush. Suddenly, drunk and high, I think I *deserve* success. Yes, I realize I'm thinking this way with *Bird Box*. Am I admitting this to myself? I don't know. Maybe I'm trying the feeling on. Right here, watching *The Evil Dead*, wanting the success these people had with this movie . . . I realize suddenly: I want a lot.

It's a dark, bad feeling. Darker than any movie I know. I believe in *Bird Box*. I believe in them all. I know it was written from a good, clean place. Yet here I am, setting myself up for some kind of linear disappointment if the book does not "succeed."

What am I doing?

"You good?" Allison asks me.

"You high?" Kenickie asks me.

"Don't ask him if he's high," Rose says. "That'll just make him twice as high."

Maybe I am a little high. Maybe I'm heading a little inward. And maybe that's why I didn't hear the knocking on the inner door. Maybe I'm standing out in the fog with the faceless man now.

Exactly what does a writer deserve?

Jesus, what a question in the middle of this movie! But also: hard not to ask it while watching the first installment of what would become such a great franchise. Watching with someone who is seeing it for the first time, giving this night at least a semblance of what it might have been like to witness it when it came out. And what was on Sam Raimi's mind after he finished filming? Did the word *deserve* cross his mind?

Whatever the reasons that word surfaced again, I don't like it. I just don't wanna think about this right now. I try to push it away.

"I'm good," I say.

But I'm still weaving in and out of these thoughts.

It's the linear versus the phenomenological. Again. Details and history, strategy and definitives, versus *experience*, the present, the now. If you set out along an artistic path because stories turn you on, because they touch a nerve only stories can touch, then your chances of success are great. Because success is the writing itself. Right? When you finish a story, you might feel you've fallen short of some ideal, but at least you'll have given yourself the chance. And it's the agency, *your* agency, for having taken that chance, that propels you from one project to the next. And the next from there.

I think so . . . yes . . . I think so . . .

Hard to say. Even here in the palms of young love and a first book deal, I'm struggling to decide what success really is. Do I fault a writer who sets out to make money? Who sees it as punching the clock, putting food on the table? No, I don't. Right? Or do I? Maybe I do. I can't tell. Maybe

I'm discovering that not only is the money mindset unrelatable (this I've known for a long time now), but I actually dislike it.

Looking at Allison, watching her watching *The Evil Dead*, it's impossible for me not to equate my relationship with writing to my relationship with her. In both cases, I need to listen to what both have to say. In both cases, I have a real and urgent desire to treat the relationship well, the bonds themselves, because I don't want to mess up a thing I've seen the best of. And that's it, isn't it? Seeing behind the curtain of real love, real drive. Until you step backstage, until you're actually watching the sandbags lifted to the wooden rafters, until you witness the actors rushing for a costume change, hearing, smelling, seeing, feeling the tension of the production behind the scenes, until then you don't really know what love is. I've stood there with Allison. I feel like I *met* her backstage, despite her having the talent, the mind, the face to be the star onstage. And I'm thinking it was her production, her existence, her life, I met her on. Just as I've wandered onto the stage of so many books I might write.

The word I think of is *respect*. Even as the movie plays with a sense of irreverence from every camera shot, every line of dialogue, every practical effect. These guys, Sam Raimi and company, these guys *respected* the art of making movies. I have no doubt of this as we watch. Passion doesn't have to be loud to be heard, but in the case of this film it's an ecstatic shout.

Still, quiet is okay. So long as you and your colors aren't muted.

I look to Rose, to Kenickie. I'm a little stoned, yes, so I don't wanna stare, don't want them to catch me staring. But I wonder: Are their colors muted? And have they forgotten to respect the bond between them, or have they reached a natural end of a natural arc?

Is there a difference?

And what is my arc with Allison? It feels the same as my arc with writing: eternal. No bend in the arc, save the work we will have to do. Naïveté and optimism are not the same thing. The naïve person doesn't know the score. The optimist knows it and chooses to do the work anyway.

I don't want to enter my relationship with Allison naïve.

I don't want to enter my career as a published author naïve.

But I also don't want to become cynical.

I want to treat everything, everybody, with respect.

Man . . .

I remember the day the High Strung set out on what would become a six-year tour. We had a meeting as we packed the bus. We thought we were facing a few months' journey, not knowing we would continue to book shows as we went, build the bridge as we crossed it. We talked about how what we were doing was unnatural. Friends see a lot of each other, but not all day every day. But out in that bus, we'd likely see sides of each other we never would have if we only met up Fridays for drinks. We were likely going to overhear phone conversations with significant others that would've been held in private. We'd get on each other's nerves. We might even fight. With fists (we did). But no matter what was to happen out there on the road, no matter what we'd find, we had to remember the reason we were setting out was because we each loved our roles in the *band*. The band had to come first. We had to listen to what the band told us to do.

Respect . . . optimism . . . knowing the score . . . listening to the work of art . . .

Sacrifices were made for the band. Romantic relationships lost. Comfort. Money. But come on, how much gained?

Everything!

Respect, yes. And embracing the experience over the strategy. Success, then, to me, was maintaining the love and care I'd started the journey with.

"Uh-oh," Rose says.

Meanwhile, Cheryl's out in the woods. Shouting, asking if anyone's out there.

"What's she doing?" Allison asks. "It's not safe!"

I love it.

Kenickie and Rose are quiet now. Those of us who have seen it, we know what's coming. The first of Sam Raimi's stop-motion effects. Iconic imagery: the tree branches attack Cheryl. And man, they're really attacking. You gotta think: At this point they knew what they had. Right? At this point they knew they were making a movie that had never been seen before.

"Holy shit," Rose says. "This is the greatest."

Because even if we've seen it, we hadn't seen it yet *tonight*.

The screaming is so '80s. The look, the sound, the wind. But not the effects. I mean, yes and no. But they're timeless.

Oh, hey she got away.

And this unbelievable aerial shot of her grabbing for the keys above the door.

Not a shot wasted with these guys.

And the first sign of comedy? The demon's groaning as she gets away.

When the three characters hand off the dialogue, *Cheryl, Cheryl, Cheryl, there's nothing out there*, Allison and I start laughing. It sounded like a little song. So we're singing it.

"Cheryl, Cheryl, Cheryl . . . there's nothing . . . out there."

We're singing it together, harmonizing. We can't stop.

Kenickie hits Pause.

"Drinks," he says.

Yes, very good idea. But Allison and I aren't done. Can't stop.

"Cheryl, Cheryl, Cheryl, there's nothing out there!"

We're singing it as we walk to the kitchen. Is there music

playing? I think Rose put the radio on. Clip is on the couch now, on his own. Rose is up, with us. All of us in the kitchen.

The smoke from the joint's as thick as the fog in *The Evil Dead*.

"Jack and Coke, baby!" Kenickie says.

He hands me one.

"And tequila and soda for you, Al."

The four of us are in the *Evil Dead* mood now. Grass as thick as fog, yes. Thoughts of branches attacking a woman. And that tune . . . we can't stop singing it.

"Cheryl, Cheryl, Cheryl, there's nothing . . . out there!"

"You two are peas in a pod," Rose says.

"Yeah?" Kenickie says. "And what are we?"

"We're two astronauts stuck in a pod, floating into space without a mother ship."

"No shit to that."

They clink glasses.

We all do.

Kenickie lights up another joint. Hands it to me. I take a hit.

Shit.

He heads outside to get some air, and I follow. As the back door closes I see Allison smiling at me. Rose is talking about how Kenickie should've straightened the place up and Kenickie is already lighting up another joint by the garbage cans outside, and *The Evil Dead* is on the brain, but Allison looks like she's lit for a movie of her own.

Sometimes I watch her sleep. I've never seen someone look so peaceful as they sleep. The tiniest hint of a smile on her face. Usually, people look a little vulnerable when they're dreaming. I know I do. Their mouth hangs open, they breathe hard. But Allison looks like a portrait. Frederic Leighton's *Flaming June*. Years later, I will still watch her sleep. As she goes to bed at seven A.M. or sometimes later, after doing woodwork with a chainsaw out in the yard or painting or listening to an audiobook. I'll go to sleep around one A.M. in those days, and our different sleep schedules will almost seem like day jobs in how they give us a few hours of alone time to do the things we do. I will write in the afternoons as she sleeps. She will work deep into the night. We'll meet in the middle.

"She keeps nagging me like a bad ankle," Kenickie says when I get to where he is.

"I guess I noticed, yeah," I say. "I'm sure it'll work out."

I'm not sure why I said this. Do I believe it?

He laughs. "That ship has sailed, my man. Dark waves now. I can't even see a foot deep into the water we're treading. I'm breaking up with her tomorrow. Or maybe she's breaking up with me tonight."

"Whoa."

"Yeah, well, you don't put me down in front of my cousin and her boyfriend. You know? Who needs it? If you're at that point in a relationship, there's no relationship to save."

"I've had rough ones too."

"Who hasn't?"

I'm a little higher now, and I'm still equating all this to a relationship with writing. I'm listening to Kenickie but I'm also seeing this parallel. I don't think I'll ever be able to untwist the fact I met Allison only months before getting a book deal. The timing, the lucky charm of her; who could extricate the two?

Who would want to?

"If you wanna be in a relationship," Kenickie says, "you gotta be prepared to apologize for things you didn't do."

I smile because I don't know why. Because we're two men smoking grass by a garbage can, and I guess what he's saying has occurred to me before.

"But I don't wanna do that," I say.

"No shit," he says. "Nobody does. But them's the rules. Either you apologize for shit you didn't do, or you're one of those guys who believes they can figure women out, and I'd rather feel the shame of the former than the madness of the latter."

"Sorry, man," I say. Then: "But you know . . . I'm thrilled for you."

He laughs.

"Really," I say. "Because it means a new phase is coming. You can do anything, be anyone."

We're quiet a moment.

"Yeah, well, I ain't gonna be dating anybody else anytime soon, that's for sure," he says. He puffs on the joint. "Hey, talk about new phases, you just crossed the finish line, you must be feeling like a totally new man."

I smile and make to say "yeah" but stop myself.

Finish line.

What a phrase at a time like this! Here I feel like the entire world is opening up and Allison's cousin just referred to a book deal as the finish line. I'm thinking about the novels I've already written. I'm thinking of the years living in friends' basements and hallways. I'm thinking of the four novels I failed to write before the ones I didn't fail to write. I'm thinking of two thousand rock shows across America, circling the country like adrenaline junkies, me in the passenger seat, a pillow under the computer open on my lap. I can still hear the Grateful Dead playing, Jerry Garcia singing, as I'm trying to write the scariest scenes I can. I'm trying to touch that nerve too. I'm thinking of *Bird Box* and how the book's no better to me, and no worse, than any of the others. Yet here she's carried me over . . .

"Not a finish line," I say. "No. This is more like day one."

"Dude," he says. "*Yeah.* Dude, you're right. It's just the start, isn't it . . ."

"Of a new phase," I say.

And it feels like we're both on the cusp of change. It feels like all four people who have gathered to watch *The Evil Dead* tonight are on the cusp of big change. Just like the five characters in the movie are about to go through some changes of their own.

I'm high, so I repeat myself. Or maybe I rewrite what I've said.

"A book deal is day one of the career. I hate the word *hobby*. Can't stand when someone says writing is a hobby. Yet, it also wasn't a *career* until now. Still . . ." I'm fumbling, trying to articulate all this. "Still, I don't see it as a career even now."

"But it is, man, and you should."

"I should, yeah. You're right. But . . . I can't let it turn into that."

"Well, you gotta be true to yourself."

"I can't start changing how I do things now."

"But like you said, change is good."

"True."

"And maybe now that you got this stuff going on, you need to think more strategically."

A memory comes to mind. It's a couple years back. I'm at the neighborhood bar I told you about, the Berkley Front. An old friend stops in, middle of the day. This friend, she's not the type to frequent bars, definitely not under the sun. How did she know to find me here? It's worrisome, this. But that doesn't matter right now.

What matters is: We sit at a high-top. I can still see that daylight coming in through the front glass behind her. She clears her throat; I'm not sure where this is going.

She tells me I need a plan B. She says, Hey, you've written all these songs, these albums, played all these shows, and written all these books . . . but nothing's happened for you. No career, no money, nothing. She lays it on strong. She's worried about me. Real worried. I recall a story my dad told me: He was a few years out of high school and a friend, also a woman, saw him at a gas station and told him he needed to get his shit in order. Needed to stop gambling and actually start making a life for himself. My dad did. I worry, at that high-top, if this is my version of that moment. But I'm not a few years out of high school. It's closer to eighteen. Still, the phrase, a cliché, of course, but heard in this context, aimed at me:

Plan B.

And she's going on and I'm thinking . . . There isn't a plan A. I'm thinking none of this is a plan at all.

I tell her as much. And I don't hate her for saying what she said. Imagine it from her angle: a good friend from grade school, dude's written a dozen novels, toured a thousand cities, drunk every time she sees him. But even then, ambushed, in a sense, by a good, smart friend with good intentions. Even then . . .

"I worry," I tell Kenickie. Maybe it's the grass. I think on a different night I might've said "yeah" or "fuck that" or just kept it short. But not this night. This night of watching *The Evil Dead*. I say, "I don't wanna discover in a few years I turned my back on something that was working." But this isn't really what I mean either. *Working* implies the goal was to get a book deal. That whatever I had in mind *worked*. "Whatever it is, right now, however I'm doing it, every time I sit down to write I'm excited. It's hard to articulate. I can't lose that."

"Funny, that," he says. "The one thing a writer can't explain is the writing."

Rose yells from inside. "Come on, you guys! We got the rest of the movie to watch!"

Kenickie huffs. But I'm with her. Let's get back to the movie.

"Whatever you do, I'm sure you'll do it right," he says.

But I'm not sure of this. And as we walk back inside, I'm feeling anxious. Maybe I shouldn't have taken another hit. Maybe what Kenickie is saying is right. Maybe just because something got you from point A to point B, it doesn't mean you're supposed to stick with it.

But that doesn't feel right either. Even just considering changing things up scares me. All that writing, tucked away in a safe room. I don't wanna go into that room with a clipboard and a whistle. I don't wanna touch it in any way I haven't touched it before. Could I imagine myself sitting down to intentionally write something that sells? No.

But can I?

No.

But come on.

No.

But doesn't that sound stubborn?

No. It's not a matter of disliking what sells. It's not a matter of fearing "selling out." It's a matter of intention, motivation, and all that can be felt on the page. You wanna talk about respecting the reader? First, trust they're going to feel where you're coming from; readers will feel what you put on the page. Even if you're setting out to write a hit, even if you succeed at that, it will be felt. But if you wanna touch that nerve, the spot inside the reader you'd only otherwise be able to touch if you were sitting at the bar together, your mutual presences felt, your energies side by side, if you want a reader to feel you, to know you, to understand you . . . you gotta write from the place that would thrill you as a reader first. You gotta get *that* on the page.

"Baby?"

It's Allison. She's found me standing alone in the kitchen. Rose and Kenickie are bickering in the living room. I think to tell Allison I was in here to fix myself a drink, but that's not true. I'm holding a full one still. She caught me thinking, is all.

"Ready?" she asks.

"Yeah."

But I wanna say so much to her. I wanna take her by the hand and tell her I want this moment in time to stay fixed forever. I want us to be young and in love forever and I want me to have just got a book deal, forever. This moment in life, without the results of either path known, I want this moment fixed forever. May *Bird Box* become the biggest horror novel of all time, may it go unnoticed, may Allison and I have twenty-five kids, may we have none, I want this moment, as it is, fixed forever. May we see the world, live in Italy, move to Finland, become puppeteers, I want this feeling to last forever.

I take her hand.

"You're stoned," she says. "Let's watch the rest."

And two things strike me.

One, Ash's friends haven't turned yet. We have a long way to go.

And two . . .

I *can* fix this night. Into forever. I can actually make that happen.

All I gotta do is . . .

Write it down.

Allison leads me back into the living room, where Kenickie and Rose are still arguing. Clip is on the couch and I pick him up and put him on my lap and Allison says, "All right, everyone. Let's shut up and do it!"

And it's funny. Because she's right. Everybody should shut up.

And everybody should do it.

"I feel like we should start over," Rose says.

I start to think how loaded this statement feels, but before I can, Kenickie says, "Not a chance."

And before I know it, we've returned to *The Evil Dead*.

A PROJECT CROSSING THE PRAIRIE, A BOOK IN THE HOUSE

Ash is alone in the basement listening to the reel-to-reel now.

They're guessing cards.

And . . .

Well, holy shit. Our first demon. And our first real demon voice.

Rose and Kenickie's living room blazes zoetic with all this color and sound. Allison is wide-eyed, glued. There's study in her gaze. She isn't just watching. She's inside this thing. The rising strings. The angles. The effects. The makeup. Allison does creature effects herself. Dozens of projects all around our house. I'm already calling her the Woman of a Thousand Faces at this point. I sense another thousand to come.

The shots. Every fuckin' camera shot. And why does the wood of the cellar door look so good? Why does Sam Raimi know how to shoot *everything*?

"That scene was absolutely awesome," Allison says.

She sips her tequila. I do the same with my Jack and Coke. Clip is crawling out of my lap, onto the couch.

And now this shot from in the cellar. Demon's-eye view. *For God's sake what happened to her eyes?*

"This is a dark painting," Allison says. "This movie is a dark painting in motion. That's what it is."

I almost say yeah, then realize I've never thought of the movie that way. My mind's a little blown. This is the best way of putting it, what she's said. Yes, *The Evil Dead* is a dark painting in motion.

It strikes me I'm no longer showing Allison the movie. She's now showing me.

I think of intention. I don't know that Sam Raimi would've called himself an artist. He might've. He might now. When I think "artist," I'm never thinking of the beret-wearing beatnik some people are embarrassed to connect with. I'm not hearing bellowing voices in coffee shops. I'm thinking of minds who see the world in terms of *ideas*. I'm thinking of people who are constantly turned on. I'm thinking of the moments when the mental Rolodex is spinning smoke and one of the numbers shines and I'm too heated by the premise not to write the entire book in a weekend. I'm thinking of the people I've known who run on electricity. They aren't going through a phase or punching in or just putting food on the table.

Intention!

I've never seen it as the artist's responsibility to define

the modern world. Do it, great. Don't do it, great. The only responsibility I feel is to the premise itself. Even if that idea is kaleidoscopically nuts. That responsibility is the most thrilling, the biggest. Like a palace guard's responsibility. Or the responsibility of the man who operates the boat out to Mackinac Island. Sam Raimi took care of this idea.

Yet, thinking again of their office in Ferndale, I know this movie required funding too. And that's a whole other animal.

"There is no budget for writing a book," I say.

No budget for writing a book . . .

On the screen. The lighting. The demon banging the cellar door. Ash's reaction. The demon voice.

Thank you . . .

And a sudden flourish of old-time cartoon music.

This is a dark painting in motion.

Man, this demon stuck and dying . . . in trouble now, deflating, crying. Ash not yet the badass, won't use the ax. It's okay, Scotty does.

Blood everywhere.

The entire lens: blood.

"Fuckin' A," Kenickie says. "This is the best movie of all time."

We laugh. Because we're high. And because tonight . . . it *is*.

How much of what we love comes from who we experience it with or who recommends it? What, in and of itself, is good, and what is not? We've all seen movies the world loved and we thought they were terrible. True of books, songs, paintings. This is not new turf. But had we stood before a painting with our mothers when we were children, had we discussed it with the person we were just falling in love with, had we taken a pic in front of it with your entire high school marching band, would our opinion of the work change?

And are we factoring in these impossible-to-predict potentialities when we consider our own art? Do we give ourselves the same room to breathe? The same chance to mean something, to different people, different combinations of people, in different circumstances?

All these thoughts are swirling as a dismembered demon trembles on the cabin floor, as Scotty tosses the ax. I love the long take following this first kill. Ash and Scotty assimilating this new reality. What did people think of this movie in 1981? It's one of the reasons I like to get the original paperback of a horror novel if I can. To feel as closely to what people felt when it came out. To see the same font. To touch the same paper. To turn the page in the middle of the same sentence. To be there as best I can.

"This is an origin story," Kenickie says. "Ash becomes, like, a superhero later on."

He does. A demon fighter. The face of fighting demons. Years later, I will read *If Chins Could Kill,* Bruce Campbell's autobiography, out loud to Allison. We'll also go see him present *The Evil Dead* at the Redford Theatre. And

Kenickie is right. One by one, Ash's friends are turning into demons and he's going to have to kill his way out of this. We've got Shelly in pieces, Linda in white, giggling, Cheryl looking out from under the cellar door, and now Scotty doesn't look so good on the couch. Ash slaps the giggling demon. Scotty says to kill her.

Yet somehow this feels more like chaos than brutality. More playful than harrowing. Like Allison said: a dark painting in motion, rather than a snapshot of mankind's worst impulses.

You know what this movie is? This movie is fun.

How many revelations, inspirations, can be found in this one movie? We're an hour deep and all I wanna do is make something myself. Sam Raimi may have been looking to entertain (I don't know), but he no doubt inspired thousands of horror fans (and artists), each of us taking something a little different from *The Evil Dead*.

What are you taking?

For me, it's that spirit, in every shot. It's the fact that, in 1981, a movie like this must've leapt from the screen. It still does. It's the idea of a group of friends working outside a system, any system, still trying to find distribution after making a movie this original. For years this movie (and this night) will be a landmark for me, a reminder that we don't know where our creations will end up, but that we gotta create them anyway. And if we work with regularity, we can look back, at any point in our lives, and see that, despite frustrations and fears, we accomplished something.

For some, this might be good parenting. Others, doing their job well. I don't know where Sam Raimi was in his life when he made this movie. My gut tells me he was in a good place. Young, energized, revved . . . but what do I know? Regardless, he'll always have this movie. And he would've had it whether it was distributed or not. It's unsettling (and fascinating) to imagine a world in which they did not find that distribution. A world in which, say, they weren't even driven to look for it. What might Sam Raimi think of the movie he'd made with friends in the woods of Tennessee if it never saw a theater screen? Would it remain a point of pride? I bet it would. It'd have to. We've all got stuff without a home. And we've all got ideas, too, bulging from our brains, each idea with fists, fighting its way out, vying for room, until, for whatever reason, we as the creators, we say *you* and *now* and we do it: we write that book, we make that album, we start that band, we film that scene.

Isn't it awesome? There may be deadlines, but how often is there a start date? Those are usually up to us. I've been talking about writing *Watching Evil Dead* for close to twelve years now. What a night! Friends, colleagues visiting my office would ask about projects-to-be. Sometimes I'd tell them about that night. About the mammoth backdrops hanging like castle regalia in the halls of my memory. Young love, old love, horror, genre, art, family, friends, creation, career, success . . .

No force outside myself told me now was the moment,

just as no studio head told Sam Raimi he had to make *The Evil Dead* on whatever date he called action. But you can feel it, can't you? When the project has begun. A loon call from across the lake. Your lake. A starting gun. You can hear it on the wind, a project crossing the prairie, a book in the house. You could be on the phone in your office, lying in bed, standing outside in the yard . . . you hear it. It's here.

Who is this?

It's you, ready now. Ready to tackle the project that, likely, started to feel like a ton of work. Started to become mythical, even to you. *Oh yes, one day I'll make that documentary. One day I'll start recording that song.* You talked about it so much and thought about it so much it became synonymous with limbo; it lived in a land called One Day, until suddenly, without warning, you discover the train you've been riding has actually made a stop in One Day, and so here you are, and the project doesn't look so big. In fact, it seems unfathomably small. *Is it possible?* you wonder. But you know the answer. You've done this before. You've been on the phone with this scenario before. Now that phone call is interrupted by the creaking of something not only in the house but much closer than that: right next to your office chair.

It's Time. And the meeting of Time and Project. And once it begins, there is no stopping it.

"Fuck yeah," I say. "There's no stopping it!" But they think I mean the movie.

Did Sam Raimi feel something like this when he got serious about *The Evil Dead*? Even the artist who creates regularly needs to be reminded that creation begins with pen to paper. Creation begins when you check in to the hotel in One Day, nothing but a suitcase on your person, already looking for locals to ask where the camera shop is, the typewriter store, the guitar and microphone too.

And the minute you arrive you realize: One Day is a lot closer than it looked on the map. You could've rolled into this town right out of bed.

So why do we wait?

But there are too many good answers to that question. Kids, work, internal insanities, external inanities, many more. For some, there's doubt, for others there's distraction, and even for some there's . . .

. . . what is *deserved*.

That question is starting to drive me nuts. We're having a party here, and it keeps creeping in like an obligation. A book report. A word I need to define before I can step into the future. It's almost making me mad at this point. I tell myself to let it go. Whatever it is. Let's answer this later. Tonight, let's horror! But the question is not going away. It's getting bigger. Louder. It's starting to feel like I'm facing something I need to face. Like I've been on a quest I knew nothing about for decades, and here I've finally come face-to-face with my foil.

"What is deserved . . ." I say.

But they don't hear me. They're engrossed. So am I.

Still . . .

Okay. If I'm face-to-face, then I'll face it.

What *is* deserved. Readership? A living? Notoriety? Sales? Likes? A figurine made in my likeness? The book on a bookstore shelf in Austria? Satisfaction? Happiness? Nirvana?

Everybody deserves everything. Right? Every living thing on Earth deserves all they desire. Right? Well, yes. But it's more complex than that. Even high with the latest hit off the joint I understand that much. Yet I keep repeating the same unintelligent platitudes to myself. It's starting to feel like this question is a trick. Like, the moment I think my book deserves anything is the moment I'm not coming from the same place I once was.

Like I'm being tricked into valuing the wrong things.

I try to remember if I used to ask myself this question driving around the country with the band. Did I ask myself what was deserved? I only remember writing songs and books.

But hang on.

Ash just found a chainsaw.

This is a big fuckin' moment.

"And here we go," Rose says.

"Oh," Allison says. "*This* scene."

Because she's seen Ash with a chainsaw before. Who hasn't? And what an interesting experience for her, tonight: seeing for herself a moment in film history that's already iconic. Almost impossible to match the myth of it.

Oh no! The cellar door is open! All these close-ups on the eyes! The music! The smoke!

"It's Grand Guignol," I say. Because I've read a couple great books on the French theater, and I don't think I've ever seen anything that comes as close to its descriptions as this movie. "Practical effects. A black-box theater."

A dark painting, in motion.

Are there frames per second removed from the film? What gives the movie its almost animated feel? I don't mean just the stop-motion stuff. But the whole movie, really. I gotta look into this. And I'm thinking *The Evil Dead* must have had a thin script. How much dialogue is even in this movie? What did they use, a thirty-page quasi-story? Imagine if you'd only read the script of this movie. Imagine if you'd never seen these images but had only read the script. They drive, they get stuck on the bridge, they get to the cabin, weirdness erupts. The book, the tape, then: demons, banging on a cellar door. That's enough for me to start with, for sure. But there's a lesson here, a big one: if *The Evil Dead* isn't much on paper—that is, not much until it was filmed—maybe we should reconsider our own ideas that feel "not enough" before they're realized too.

After all: once you *do*, you *are*.

Once you write it down, you've shown yourself how it can be done. You've seen behind the lines, behind the curtain, over the mountain. Now, and only now, you can make it great. But you gotta see an idea played out before you know how "enough" it is.

Before you present it to anybody else, you get to present it to yourself.

Exciting thoughts, these. Puts every idea you've got in play. Nothing's dismissed. There's a reason the idea thrilled you to begin with. In the moment of its inception, you saw how it could be done. And maybe, if you're doubting it now, maybe you've just forgotten.

"Ah, come on, don't go down there," Allison says.

Ash standing in the open door to the cellar now.

Allison, so into it.

"Don't worry," Rose says. "He doesn't."

"Rose," Kenickie says. "Don't spoil it. Why you gotta spoil things?"

"It's okay," Allison says. "I look things up all the time."

"I do not *spoil* things," Rose says.

Ash is pounding demons onscreen. Old friends of his are wheezing.

"That's exactly what you do," Kenickie says. "You take a thing and you spoil it."

"You think I don't know not to spoil something?" Rose says.

Voices rising now. We're all a little drunk.

Meanwhile Ash *is* going down into the basement. So, I don't even know what was spoiled.

Allison is completely enthralled.

Pipes bursting with blood. Lightbulbs filling up with blood.

"You *spoil* things," Kenickie says. "The dog is spoiled, and we've had it for three days."

I look down. The dog is in my lap again, looking back up at me.

Madness here at the end of the movie now. Amazing shots. Spinning dolly shots. Ash upside down. That incredible swooping in time with the descending violins. Iconic underlit shot of Ash.

Who thought to use that blue shirt for Ash? Could they have known how iconic even this shirt would become? Was this a small decision? A big one? I can't help but guess Sam Raimi was going on instinct. But not with the lenses. Not with the incredible effects. All of it screams of someone who's been working toward this moment. A brilliant combination of wholly freeing his spirit but also totally knowing his gear.

I'm thinking about "working toward this moment." I'm supposed to go to New York City soon, to "present" *Bird Box* to the press. Reps from *USA Today* will be there. *People, The New York Times Book Review.* ECCO/HarperCollins is really pushing this book. Two other debut authors will be there too. I suddenly get nervous about this. High and drunk, watching *The Evil Dead,* I suddenly imagine myself at the Museum of Modern Art, talking to these luminaries of book reviewing.

I am so new to this, I don't even know how new I am.

Almost a year from now, I will be packing my suitcase

when I receive an email from the publisher, reminding me I'm supposed to give a speech about *Bird Box* at the visit to MoMA. I didn't know this was supposed to happen. I will freak the fuck out, imagining myself standing in front of those critics from famous publications, me, a Michigander with little history of public speaking, little history of "giving speeches," doing so at one of the most fabled museums in New York City. The night before the event, already in the city, Allison and I will be in a red booth in a vegetarian restaurant in Greenwich Village. I will start shaking, unable to stand up, so scared to do this, and the red booth will have me feeling like I'm in the lap of the devil.

A speech. About my book.

The next morning, early, I will be crying in the hotel room. So scared. Allison will tell me to drink an airplane bottle of booze from the room's little refrigerator. She will tuck another one in my suit jacket pocket.

And minutes before I'm to deliver this speech, standing in front of three dozen members of the press, standing before a ten-foot poster of the cover art for *Bird Box,* I will learn that one of the fellow debut authors, Smith Henderson, took ten years to write his first novel. It will calm me down, this fact. The different paths people can take to arrive at the same exact moment in time. More than a dozen novels for me, one for him, the two of us debuting together. Smith will give his speech first. It will be like watching a fellow prisoner perform for the king. He looks as nervous as I feel. This will calm me down too. And when my turn comes, I will rush through a handful of ill-prepared sentences that will haunt me for years to come. It was as if Smith and I decayed in stop-motion animation.

Still, we did it.

But I'm a long way from doing it while we watch *The Evil Dead*.

Ash throws the book on the fire.

The demons stop moving.

The music stops.

"Did I *spoil* this?" Rose asks Kenickie.

Huffing. The two of them.

And the stop-motion decay. The colors. The expression on Ash's face.

If the world hadn't noticed a fresh voice in the movie's first seventy-eight minutes, they sure as shit saw it now.

Allison and I can't sit still. We barely hear Rose and Kenickie fighting.

Hands erupting from the decaying bodies!

The bugs!

Ash splattered in blood and guts . . .

Is this the greatest ending of all time?

"Triumphant, covered in blood . . ."

Who said that? Rose? Allison? Me?

"I feel like we've seen Bruce Campbell become a better actor," Allison says. "*As* the movie went on."

"It's not over yet!" Rose says.

This bothers Kenickie.

Now, on the screen, it's day. The whole movie was one

night in the cabin, fighting demons. Ash has seen some shit now. Done some shit too.

The sun is up in *The Evil Dead*.

Ash, covered in blood, exits the cabin. Closes the door behind him. That's funny to me.

Swelling, romantic music.

And this, the last shot. Absolutely brilliant. Starts on a close-up of a leaf, then pans low through the woods, fast now, through the cabin itself, out the front door, and . . .

"*No way,*" Allison says.

As . . .

Ash screams.

Cut.

Written and directed by Sam Raimi.

We all breathe out. I turn to Allison.

"That was even better than expected," she says. "That was . . . I need a second before I say what that was."

And we take that second, all of us.

Then we're all up, heading for the kitchen. The old swing music is playing during the credits. But these are short.

"Refills," Kenickie says.

"You sure you need more?" Rose asks him.

I'm thinking of the fact this movie existed before it had distribution. That it existed, finished, before the world saw it. Think: There are moments in time when the classics are done, the work is finished, but the world has yet to experience them; still secret. When Marcel Proust finished writing *Swann's Way,* only he knew what it was. I think of that moment, that beat (and this kind of a beat can last months, years), as a sort of forever. The moment in time when nobody knew what *The Evil Dead* was . . . yet it did exist, just as much as it exists now. It may feel like a meek philosophical question, but it's worth asking: if the world hasn't yet agreed a work of art is a classic, is it still a classic? *The Evil Dead* existed and was likely physically in that office in that building Allison and I visited. An absolute landmark of cinema history, just sitting in metal canisters on what I imagine to be a chipped wooden desk. A landline at hand. Papers, smoke, pens and pencils, phone numbers, addresses, notes. The movie existed there just as your book may exist, sitting on your desk, unread, so far.

For this: We can't (it'd be insane to) judge what we do by views, likes, reviews. Because that movie Allison and I just watched with Kenickie and Rose, *that* movie was once finished and inert, sitting in exactly the same place all our work goes. Even if it's only temporarily there, everything we do ends up on the same platform, waiting for its train. And does the train always come? And if so, how fast? When? But these questions are trivial. Because the classics spent time at the station too. You see?

"I love you," Allison tells me. "And I love this night."

"Happy hour," Kenickie says, handing us fresh drinks. "And cheers to Sam Raimi."

We all toast to Sam Raimi.

"All right," Rose says. "Are you guys ready?"

I'm wiping whiskey from my lips.

"Ready for what?" I ask.

She smiles; her eyes get small and evil behind her glasses.

"The remake."

THE BALLAD OF LAURENCE URDANG

ALLISON AND I HAVE A minute alone before we start the re-make. Kenickie and Rose are in a room up the hall. We've reached that point in the night where the couple who's arguing decides to take a moment and do it alone. We can hear them, and I'm thinking of arcs again, the arcs of love and interests.

"We can do something like that movie," Allison says. "You write it, I'll star. I can do the effects. We need to do something."

I feel it too. But hearing her say it is powerful. The Woman of a Thousand Faces has shown she can do anything with makeup and effects. And if she did star, she could be anything, anybody.

A year from now, we will make that potty-humor movie, *Jizzly Bear.* I'll wonder how much of it was influenced by this night. While it's nothing like *The Evil Dead*, there's a buoyancy to the shots, the edits, the music. An animated feel that intentionally undercuts any realism (to say the least). Allison will play a man in the movie, a guy who masturbates in a deer blind and accidentally impregnates a bear. Five years later, a young man-bear torments the town in which Sam (Allison) lives. With the help of Sam's friends, cynical Burt (Eric Kozlowski), who carries a saber, and wide-eyed Allan (Jason Glasgow), who wears a pile of shit on his head (think *poopee* rather than *toupee*), Sam will track Jizzly Bear down and confront his only child in the grossest bear den you've ever seen. I'll write and direct. Allison will star, do all the effects, makeup, more. We'll find and edit the classical music together. This will be my first project following the biggest (and at the time only) book release of my life. My friend Phil Doherty will point this out to me. Soon I'll understand this is no accident: after near breakdowns like I had at MoMA, I'll need the DIY soul of *Jizzly Bear*. While it will be the craziest thing Allison and I have done, it will also be something we quietly acknowledge through the years; a smile across a dinner table if someone says anything that resembles a line from the movie; endless quoting in our own house; endless screenings for friends, drunk, late at night at our place. We'll end up premiering the movie at a local art house, one showing, nearly three hundred people, mostly rock 'n' rollers, artists, writers, and two of our closest friends will meet that night, fall in love, and marry.

There are always these magical stories surrounding the works of art you do "for no reason." Always these memories. It's like life understands when you stretch, it sees you have more room in you now, decides to use that space.

Still, I'll know Allison means something other than *Jizzly Bear* when she says this to me after we watch *The Evil Dead*. And by the time I begin to write about this night, we'll be juggling three potential movies we wanna make.

Hold me to them, please.

"I was expecting that to be more of a comedy," she says.

"That's part two. It's like a living cartoon. If I'm remembering it right."

We kiss. We hear Rose and Kenickie still arguing up the hall.

"Guess we're sleeping here," she says.

We both look to the couch, where Clip sits alone.

"Drunk," we both say at once.

Clip nods. Like he knows this already. Allison and I laugh. And we can't stop. And I wonder if the couple up the hall hear us like an echo of the beginning of their arc. Is the sound cruel to them? Does it remind them of something they (possibly even recently) forgot?

Watching Allison, I have a sudden overwhelming understanding that she is my friend.

"I felt like you showed *me* that movie," I tell her.

"Aw. That makes me wanna have kids."

"What?"

"Maybe I'd be the kind of mom to show our kid *The Evil Dead*."

Kenickie and Rose come down the hall. Allison fauxshrieks because we did just watch a horror movie and there are suddenly two people beside us.

"Wanna step outside?" Kenickie asks us.

I go. Allison stays. She and Rose talk about Clip and how Rose might wanna keep him after all, and Allison is saying she wants to get a Weimaraner and I'm calling over my shoulder, "You know, we don't *have* to add another neurotic entity to the house."

I must be higher than I think because Kenickie and I are standing by the garbage cans again, and I barely remember exiting the back door.

"Shit's nuts," he says. "Constant shit."

"I'm sorry, man."

"Don't be. We do it to ourselves. Right? We want love, we find it, but then we're all pissy when it goes sideways. Are your parents divorced?"

"Dude, I was *just* thinking about that. Yes."

"Yeah, well, we probably sparked that thought. How many relationships have you had before Allison?"

I have to think about this. "I mean, since seventh grade?"

"Sure. Since then."

"Maybe . . . five?"

"All right, and you're batting a thousand in your relationships going sideways. That's what people forget, man. No matter who you're dating now, that means all your relationships before this one failed."

"Failed," I say. "I've never thought of it like that."

"Yeah, well, you thought you were living in forever with each of them. But then . . ." He fans a hand to the back door. "The day comes where you can't stop embarrassing yourself."

"Well, don't worry about us."

"But that's just it," he says. He lights up another joint. "The emotions are so strong you don't even care who's there to see it. In fact, *in fact,* you're feeling so righteous, you kinda *want* friends and family to see it. So, they can tell you you're right. Do you think I'm right?"

"About what?"

"Does it seem like I'm doing anything wrong? Am I starting shit?"

I don't know what to say. I hadn't thought about who was right or wrong. But I know the feeling.

"No," I say. "I don't think so. No."

"Is she? Man. Maybe I'm the one who's fucked."

"There's a reason you're dating her in the first place. She's cool. You wouldn't be dating her if she wasn't. But like, that doesn't mean you should be dating."

"*Right.*"

"I try to stay friendly, if not friends, with my exes. Because, you know, there was a time we saw something really good in each other. Just because we split doesn't mean one of us sucked."

"But it sure as shit feels like it at the time."

"It does."

I'm thinking how easily relatable this is to writing. Early love is like the rough draft. So many errors, happily overlooked, practically floating through the experience of getting the story on paper. Who cares how much is right or wrong in the rough draft, in the early days of love? We can rewrite it later. We can fix shit down the road. Years from now, with better perspective. And here's a guy who once loved, now maybe doesn't but will no doubt one day recall bits of vitality, some good, in what he had with Rose.

I take another hit. This is getting stupid at this point. I barely held on through the end of the first movie, I can only imagine what's to come.

"The remake is good," he says.

"You saw it in the theater?"

"Yeah. Loud as shit. Badass."

"I'm usually last to the party," I tell him. "Can't tell you how many times I thought something was only okay, just to love it later."

And who was I when I first watched *The Evil Dead*? Was I someone who understands the things I do now, this night, smoking grass by the garbage cans with a man who is starting the road to separation? The changes are so gradual. A word here, a word there.

"Part two is the one everyone thinks of when they talk about *Evil Dead*," Kenickie says. "Can't tell you how many motherfuckers I've had to correct. 'No, the *hand* is the second one.' Most of the time people still don't believe me."

"What year did it come out?" I ask.

"Part two? Eighty-seven."

"Six years after the first."

"Yeah, he made a movie called *Crimewave* between. You seen it?"

"No."

"We'll have to have that night next."

Then, a moment of silence and while I know we can watch a movie anytime with Kenickie, I feel like we both know that's not going to happen. He and Rose are splitting. It feels like a new path opening for him, for them both. There's no way for me to know at this moment that Kenickie will move out of town within the year.

"Six years," I say. Because I'm high and that sounds like a long time between installments. Again, years later I will release *Malorie* five years after *Bird Box*. I'll see firsthand how quickly six years can go by in the writer's life. Then again, between *Bird Box*'s release and writing *Malorie* I'll have written thirteen more novels. But I can't know this, the night we watch *Evil Dead*.

I shudder suddenly. Don't know why. Likely high. And the four or five drinks aren't repelling it. Maybe it's all the talk of sequels and people's favorites, all satellites of commercial success. *Franchises*. It's a deep fear, this, dark and strong. It suddenly feels to me that, no matter how things go, I'm not ready for them.

"You're gonna be just fine," Kenickie says.

Did he see it in my eyes? I don't think I said anything out loud. Yet, in tune. All four of us, in a strange way. It's the movie, I think, the centerpiece of the night.

We're quiet for a beat.

Then: "Thanks," I say.

"Yeah, well, don't tell Rose I'm out here being mushy. She'll get mad I'm not being mushy with her."

Loud laughter from inside, and Kenickie dabs the joint out on the grill and we head back in. Rose and Allison are lying on the floor as Clip walks all over them. He walks from Allison's toes to Allison's head, then steps onto Rose's head, then walks down to her toes, then over to Allison's toes again. The dog is doing laps on a human track.

"Get a picture of this," Rose says.

I don't have a smart phone yet. Years later I'll wish I still didn't.

But Kenickie takes pics of the dog. It's adorable. It's funny. I lie down beside them and when Clip gets down to Allison's toes, he pauses at the tip of my cowboy boot. We're all laughing. What will he do? But he goes the Rose route again.

Kenickie sets up the remake. The title art fills the screen.

Lying on the living-room carpet, I'm brought back to the video store with Mom. She's in the New Releases section and I walk away, lying to myself, telling myself I'm just looking around. But I'm heading somewhere specific.

In the private museum of all horror fans, is there any place as reverent as the memory of the horror section in the video store?

In those days, and at that age, there weren't many places to see images like these. There were a handful of magazines out at the time, but I can't imagine Mom or

Dad buying me one of those. I'm not even sure I knew what *Fangoria* was at ten years old. But the horror aisle at the video store, now, the *horror aisle:* You'd see stuff on the boxes you couldn't believe. *The Company of Wolves.* The man isn't turning into a werewolf; there's a wolf coming *out of his mouth.* And *A Nightmare on Elm Street,* where five finger-knives hover above a woman in bed. And, of course, Michael Berryman on the cover of *The Hills Have Eyes.*

We're talking root fear.

All the boxes painted or shot with that same care Allison pointed out in the movie we just watched. Dark paintings, dark art. You could frame ninety-five percent of them. I'd walk that museum every day. Mom and I used to love going to the Detroit Institute of Arts, and I'd beg her to take me to the darker stuff. Even just a shadowy oil portrait. Even then, the shadows beyond the subject thrilled me.

There was one VHS cover that followed me around the store, one I honestly avoided, or tried to, as long as I could stand it.

The living eyes in the skull on the VHS box for *Evil Dead 2* is the *Mona Lisa* of horror art.

Are the eyes upset? Or are they laughing? Are they funny? Are they deadly serious? There was no way to tell then, and it's hard to know now.

"Let's do it," I say, sitting up quick.

"Come on, Rose," Kenickie says. "You're embarrassing yourself on the floor."

"We're all on the floor!" Allison says.

"Yeah, well, she probably started it," he says.

Kenickie's in a totally different place than I am right now. Allison's mom often talks about the "seasons of love." She'll say she and Mike are "in winter" or "spring again." The first time she said it, it stuck with me. Because not only is it honest to the moment, but it also opens your thinking to the idea that things will, and do, change. And that's okay. You're feeling sour about your work? Give it a minute. Or give it a season. But know this: how you feel and what you're enduring will change. Things will change because things must change. Literally nothing remains static, nothing can. This has to include self-image, and how we see what we create.

But there's a sense here, between Kenickie and Rose, that they've moved beyond needing to give it just a season. Is this the mark of true love traveled? When the work is no longer worth it? When the memories of the highs no longer carry the lows? This decision doesn't have to come from a bad place. Nobody had to lie or cheat. Nobody had to "fail." As three of us are getting up off the floor and taking our positions on the couch and recliners again, I'm thinking how a relationship's early days act as fuel and might determine the length of the relationship to come. Not to say a stove-hot courtship equals longevity. But the honest depth of that initial stage might serve as a reminder to all involved that when things get hard, it's still worth the work.

Same with writing.

Here, like this:

Where were you coming from when you started writing? A place of devotion? Likely somewhere not easily described. Likely it was a pressing need, or even: *fun*. What moved you about the books you love? Did you picture a career of your own, built off a skill you'd develop? Did you feel a drive to tell stories like the ones you read? Did you discover a need to express yourself beyond whatever being online offers you? While I don't worship, I look up to so many writers. The tools, the voices, the ability to make quick decisions . . . it's all so hard to articulate. They must have all taught me lessons about writing, but I don't remember it that way. It feels more like they gave me the medium itself. With each book I read, I'd keep notes of two, three, four novel ideas of my own. If I thought the book was going one place but then it didn't, maybe that direction was *my* story to tell. Other times a peripheral character struck a chord. They didn't play a big role in Dickens's book, but maybe someone like them could star in mine. A part of them anyway. An occupation, a hairstyle, a middle name as a first, a first as a middle.

And so how much of this *initial* love for the medium has fueled the dozens of novels and short stories and songs that followed? How much of the current fantasy is still riding on that initial swoon, that courtship, being swept up in everything I read, that sense that, even with the books I didn't love, I somehow loved the fact I was holding any book at all?

Work. Right? In love and in art. Work. And knowing that work is coming. Being so well versed in the fact you might dislike yourself along the way that when that negativity comes, you're not surprised. The difference between being too scared to do something and just brave enough to try is garlic-slice thin. But that tiny advantage was likely forged in the days you fell in love.

Remember those days. When it comes to art. Remember those days. Because while we've all had relationships end (and many of them should've ended, all good), the relationship with writing is a relationship with ourselves. And to overcome the winter seasons will take work. It's a marriage, in the truest, oldest sense of the word.

"Here we go then," Rose says. "All you fuckers pay attention."

I didn't realize Kenickie had hit Play.

And then . . .

Presto. The movie. The remake. And from the word go it's nothing like the original. Not in feel, look, color, sound.

"The remake," I say. As if needing to understand what I'm seeing.

In a way, it's the reason we're gathered here at all. Can't watch the remake if you haven't seen the original. Well, you can. Only, Allison hadn't. The problem is, it's hard enough to watch a movie the day after you finish reading the book. Here, we've started the remake just minutes after the credits of the original *Evil Dead*. We're totally not giving the remake a chance. Add in an elephant's dose of whiskey, and there's a real loose hold on things right now.

I'd heard someone remade *The Evil Dead,* but I didn't know much more than that and my first instinct was, of course: Who needs it? And on a night like this, no less, right? The living room is a whole different experience now from how it was when we arrived. It's blurry, foggy, and has the piqued but clumsy energy of four people with a lot on our minds, both good and bad. That said, I glance up the hall past the TV and see Rose and Kenickie kissing like teenagers in the dark. I didn't even know they'd left the room.

I watch the movie. I pivot on a dime.

Why not a remake?

It strikes me that, if not the script, the concept of the original *Evil Dead* could be seen like a play. This idea, of course, could hold true of any story ever written. Are we watching a "remake," or is it just a different production of that original concept, a different troupe performing the original story? I think: *This is a different theater troupe's vision of the same story.* We've come to tie movies so deeply to money, we can barely see any motivation besides that. But we don't know the people who made this movie. And isn't *Evil Dead* a modern-day *Dracula*? *The Iliad, Arsenic and Old Lace, Macbeth* . . .

I think of Professor Barclay. The college lecture as performance art. It calms me, reminds me to think in terms of experience . . .

We're constantly leaving ourselves presents as artists. With every book we read, every conversation we have. So long as we're open to everything we take in. That includes, of course, the stuff we're ready to dismiss.

"There's no such thing as a remake," I say. A stoned flag in the sand. "It's just a different theater company in town."

I like this idea so much I say it twice to Allison, and she tells me she's the one who told me this, a couple weeks back. And, oops, she's right. We were in Marquette, Michigan, and we saw the remake of *Carrie*. She said it then. Now, stoned, drunk, inspired (and not a little worried about where the make-out session down the hall might lead; everything feels combustible), I'm imagining these actors and the director, all of them in traveling theater-troupe trailers, rolling into Royal Oak, Michigan, to perform this night, for us. Years later, Allison and I will see the thousandth run of *Hamilton* with none of the original cast and we'll think it's one of the best shows we've ever seen.

I'm imagining a theater here in town.

I'm imagining a French Grand Guignol theater.

Practical effects on a dimly lit stage. Live music: strings and timpani. All the walls painted black.

Let's scare people like it was done before moving pictures.

Suddenly I wanna buy a theater.

"You're good at talking about what you do," Allison tells me.

"So are you."

"Maybe. But it's not the same. You rev up the room with it."

I barely understand what I'm seeing on the screen. I'm thinking of Sam Raimi wrapping *The Evil Dead* and the fire he must've felt. Everyone they talked to must've been able to see it. Whether they were talking about the movie or not.

I think about what Allison just said.

Maybe it's good to talk about what you do.

And suddenly, a year from my first book being published, I realize I feel comfortable saying a writer *deserves* to talk about their book.

Phew. Okay. This feels like a start.

"Imagine Beethoven in a lantern-lit parlor, talking through what he's working on."

"Oh?" Allison says. "Is this where we're at now? Beethoven in the parlor."

I smile. "Yeah. Imagine Edward Albee outside a New York brownstone. Talking about an idea he has for four drunks . . ."

When you finish a work of art, no star pops up above your head. You aren't suddenly handed a sandwich board displaying your book's title. What you get is ardor, birr, might. It comes in the modest form of thrilling conversation. You have more pep in your step, your greens are greener, your reds a brighter red. No slump. No slouch.

Your wants are up-to-date. You are not *longing*.

You had an idea.

You wanted to write the idea.

You spent weeks, months, corralling the idea. Getting *into* writing shape as you wrote. You turned down certain nights out. You said yes to others. You wrote through hangovers and concerns, bad phone calls and good. You took a day off you didn't want to take off. Your mom called. Your dad called. Rent was due. You ate too little. Drank too much. Woke with a start; it started to feel like you were losing your mind whenever (even if it was just an hour) you weren't writing. Three weeks in, you felt you could write the whole book in five days. Then: doubts. Nasty, murderous misgivings. These ran their course. Then you saw land. You overextended yourself the last couple weeks. You caught your reflection, you saw someone gaunt, frazzled, wrecked. You winked and pressed, you pushed, you worked.

You finished the book.

Rough draft or not . . . a version of it was *done*.

Then?

Oh, then . . .

You are changed. Don't laugh. Could anyone dare argue they're the same after finishing as they were before starting? *You are changed.* In some ways big, others unrecognizably small. You're no longer consumed with vague sequences and scenes; these are written now. They are concrete, they are inked on screen or paper.

So . . .

Now you talk about it. How can you not? People meet up. They ask each other how they are. They ask each other what they've been up to. You, you've been up to your neck in letters.

You bring up the book.

Does the universe hear you? Are its winds behind you or do they blow in your face? We can all feel the momentum of the universe, whichever direction it moves. We know when things are going for or against us.

"You know," I say to Allison, "back when we lived in New York, when I was feeling particularly insane in the basement of the place we rented, I used to say, *I can write my way out of this*. The mood, the state of mind, whatever it was. *I can write my way out of this*."

As if the letters and the words themselves could become a stool, then a ladder, reaching the window up in the wall.

We could be raising kids, attending weddings, going to school, allowing a broken hand to heal . . . but no matter what we're doing, our current project is in the room with us. It doesn't poke or nag, but its presence is felt; it always makes itself known. Friends and family will ask what's on our mind. A manager at work, a co-worker, a student . . . they can all feel an idea is close. An entity in the room. Something corporeal but also not. For this, the day we begin working on our newest project, is the same day we begin climbing toward that window, knowing, believing, suddenly, that this idea will one day (and one day soon) become part of our oeuvre, our canon, our body of work. This idea, this work, will become just as much a part of us as any we've made before. That's the beauty of a body of work. Each book, song, movie is equal in representing the artist as a whole. There's a transformation with each creation. Our *persona* is altered, as we create. Our *identity* has been modified. And so then must our style, our step, our speech.

Everything about us is reborn.

By the end of an artist's body of work, they are unrecognizable if placed side by side with whoever they were when they began.

Just when you think you know yourself . . . you write another book.

Never let an idea die. A version, of course. But the idea that ignited the book or song? There was a reason it prompted an entire novel. And the ideas that spawn novels are the thumbprint of the artist. I won't turn my back on one just because I was too young to do it justice. I'll try it again.

I keep all ideas behind glass. In the office museum. In the brain. Don't let your younger self embarrass you into letting a book idea go.

"I'm glad we're watching these back-to-back," Allison says. "Feels like I'm going to *Evil Dead* school."

Years later, she will be able to recall this movie, scene by scene, whereas I'll see a couple images that broke through the mind fog of grass and Jack Daniel's.

"A guy like Sam Raimi," I say, "he's got so many good movies. Do you think he's overwhelmed with options? With what he should do next?"

Does order matter?

Spirit over strategy. Temper over trend.

How many times have you felt like not doing the thing, then you begin, you get into the groove, and find you can keep at it forever?

So, why wait?

And what really needs to be fleshed out?

The script for *The Evil Dead* didn't include the color of the blood, the look in Bruce Campbell's eyes, the actual tone and pitch of the demon voices.

Yet when the script was done, they were on their way.

I squeeze Allison's hand just as Kenickie and Rose re-enter the room. They don't look happy. I have no idea if they fought, made out, made up, or had a thumb war.

"Is it good?" Rose asks.

"We can start it over," Allison says.

"No, it's okay."

"It's good," Allison says. "It's its own thing."

She likes it. I love that she likes it.

Kenickie leans over to me, thinks he's whispering but he isn't: "You ever get writer's block?"

"What?"

"You ever get stuck?"

"Oh, well . . ." I slide nearer to where he sits in the recliner. We talk as the movie plays. "I get stuck. I guess. In a session. I think. But I just tell myself to make a sharp turn. But . . . hang on . . . let's not use me as an example." I'm stoned. "Let's not jinx me. Let's talk about a writer named . . . um . . . Frank N. Stein."

"Frankie Stein!" Kenickie laughs. "I love his stuff! Does he get stuck?"

"Frankie doesn't get writer's block. He's too busy trying to bring the different body parts to life. He's occupied, right? He's thinking . . . the state of the body, the book . . . as a whole. He can stitch it together better later."

I'm thinking of being elastic with writing. I'm thinking of tangents and how the real envelope worth pushing is mailed within yourself. To yourself. One residence (before starting a new project) to a new one (once you've begun).

"I guess you got it all figured out then," Rose says.

"Rose, lay off him," Kenickie says.

"What do you mean?" I ask.

Is she mad at me? I think of the bookseller Guppy who didn't like me.

"You just make it sound so easy," she says. "Writing books. Everyone else makes it sound like hell."

"Oh," I say. "Okay. Yeah, well, it's insane. The work. The worry. It's madness. But that's a given. I don't have kids, but I imagine it's something like that. Like, even when you're showing people the adorable pics, everyone knows you're exhausted."

"Rose," Kenickie says. "You don't think he works hard?"

"I didn't say that. Did I say that, Allison?"

"Nope. You didn't say that."

"It's okay," I say. "I don't mean to come off so . . . bright about it all. Think of it more like a guy confined to Alcatraz, but he's always got ideas on how to get out."

"So, is it escapism for you?"

"No. I don't like that way of explaining it either."

"But you just said—"

"Rose, he said no."

"Not *escapism*," I say. "It's just . . . all of us, we're all going through a lot. Whether it's family or career or dreams or whatever. Writing and reading aren't escapes for me as much as they're . . . meditative states."

But that doesn't sound right either.

"No," I say. "Not that. But *like* that. It's more like a sustained childhood. But . . . in an adult state of mind."

I'm flailing. Or am I?

"But no writer's block?"

"I don't believe in it."

"How come?"

"Because I think that's a different phrasing for self-doubt. And those doubts come from being out of shape with it. And for believing you're tethered to an arc. In your story and, I don't know, maybe outside it too. It comes from comparing what you're writing to stories you've read. Good and bad, that kind of thing."

"I don't agree. Sometimes isn't it a matter of just . . . not knowing what comes next?"

"But those are different things, right? Not knowing what comes next is not the same thing as being blocked. Not for me anyway. Uncertainty isn't a dead end. Character, setting, plot. It's a blank page, and your words . . . that's a book. Truly, anything goes. Imagine an entire novel written in pointillism, no sentences, just words. Imagine that. *Meadow. Boots. Man. Coming. Crunch. Farmhouse. Window. Widow. Phone. Knife. Cut. Phone line.* If you could write an entire book without sentences, then anything goes."

"You should do that," Allison says. "That pointillism book."

"That's insane," Kenickie says. "I love it."

He hands me the joint. I take it.

"I think some writers take greater care of their works than maybe you do," Rose says.

Kenickie coughs. "Rose!"

"I think you're totally right," I say. "But Keith Richards has a slurry guitar sound, and *Moby-Dick* is maybe bloated. I think the Rolling Stones care more about the feel, the roll, than the rock. But they also get the best sounds they can, right? I hear you. But also, however I'm doing it, I'm doing it. And that means the most to me."

In the distance I hear the word *deserve* whispered. I almost examine it. But it's carried on a cold mental wind. I don't have the space for it right now, sparring with Rose.

"It makes me take you less seriously," she says.

And I think Kenickie is gonna flip.

"Well, okay," I say. "I'm not sure how to answer that. Come hang out for a rough draft. That'll explain this better than I can tonight."

"I just want you to reveal yourself."

"Right now?"

"Right now."

Reveal yourself . . .

"It's impossible not to reveal yourself," I say. "That's what I love about it. It's redundant to 'reveal' yourself in a medium that's already naked. Like a billboard advertising billboard space."

The novel: a nude painting. Every writers' convention a nudist colony.

The novel: a lie-detector test. Every book bugged for the truth.

The novel: without makeup. No glasses or good lighting.

The novel: if done with purpose, man versus himself. If done with spite, man versus man.

The novel: a cool, solitary space (a cabin, say, in Tennessee), where only the desire to tell the story, to express, heats the space. Without *drive* . . . the writer will freeze. And we need to be fast on our feet. One-person improv troupes. We gotta handle the hurdles fast.

And if we don't? Okay. Roll the tape back, let's record a second take.

(And maybe one day Ash will listen to it.)

Why is everyone forgetting this? Why is everyone forgetting that we can fix it all, rewrite, as we go?

The novel! A bridge we build *as* we cross it. So that we're scared at first; it doesn't yet reach the other side. How can we cross this bridge if it doesn't yet exist?

But that's what we do.

Can you hear the invisible drummer? She's drumming for you. The rhythm you hear is the rhythm of your story. *Who's this in my fruit cellar?* Why, it's your drummer! And she's sweating and she's bleeding and she's so incredibly steady and if you'd just listen to her, you'd see the whole thing is mapped out for you, measure by measure . . .

"I don't think it's redundant," Rose says. "I rather like reading emotional transparency."

"But that's the novel," I say. "It's a series of photos you were nervous about. But the second they go public (and nobody's disgusted by them), you're not only okay with them, you kinda love 'em too. You now include them in your mind's eye, your self-image, your idea of yourself. We expand our idea of ourselves by writing."

"You're definitely high," Rose says.

"You are definitely right."

I am. And I feel like I've been high since the day Mark

Owen, Derek Berk, and I played songs in Derek's mom's basement, as Mark sang poems he and I had written. Our first glimpse of being a band.

When did you *know* you wanted to be a writer? Could you have known? Did the idea exist as an identity when you were a kid? Or is it the kind of thing you can only look back on, spotting the breadcrumbs along the path . . . ?

Yeah, I'm high all right, Rose. I'm back in the basement. The cellar.

"Michigan State sweatshirt," I say, pointing to the screen. "We got *Evil Dead* and Magic Johnson, and I'm not sure we need any more than that."

I wasn't expecting the remake to be as scary as it seems like it is. But the truth is, the four of us have transcended "watching." We are now riding *Evil Dead*.

"Is that why you write so much?" Kenickie asks. "Like taking pics of yourself?"

"But not selfies," I say. "A book is a two-way camera. Shots of you, shots of me, shots of everyone and everything."

Sam Raimi poured his spirit into an inanimate object: a film. And we're reaping the occult benefits tonight. We can't stop talking process.

"Okay, one more question," Rose says. "And then I'll leave you alone."

"I don't wanna be left alone," I say. "Sounds scary."

"For real. I wanna know—"

"Rose," Kenickie says. "Whatever this is, don't ask it. You're gonna fuck up the entire mood. You got us to a good spot. Let's stay there."

Rose stands up. "Fuck you, Kenickie. This is why we're breaking up. This is why we're wrong. You don't tell someone else what to say."

"When you've heard someone say it enough times . . ."

But Rose walks past us, into the kitchen. On the screen, the girl just got whooshed into demonhood as the bearded guy spoke the summoning words. I think: in any incarnation, any version put on by any traveling company, the low running shot coupled with those magic words will always thrill us.

Rose steps back into the room. "Kenickie?"

She dumps a beer on his head.

Kenickie leaps from the chair and turns on her like he's going to do something terrible. But he doesn't. And I think maybe they used to do stuff like this all the time. And I think it used to make them laugh. Pranks, scares, dumping beers on each other's heads. Rose is half-smiling like this is a final try, maybe an experiment of a sort, to see if it really is the end of them. Will he laugh? Will he get so mad he breaks the wall?

But, high and drunk, he does neither. And while Allison and I had been ready to laugh along with him, Kenickie just sits back down in the chair.

Rose, standing behind him, nods.

"Please don't do it again," Kenickie says.

And I feel I can hear it. The final cracking apart of two hearts that were once one.

I look to Allison.

What is our future? When we met, there was Allison, there was me, and there was timing. I've only been so sure of one other thing in my life. It's as if the writing of novels and songs keeps the peace on the interior while Allison patrols the exterior; a best friend, a lover. I do not tell the books what to do any more than I tell Allison what to do any more than I tell my bandmates what to play when I bring out a new song. I respect them all the same. For this, the body of work, and my relationship with Allison, will develop over the years spanning forward from this night of watching *Evil Dead*. I will never cheat on the books, nor would I ever cheat on Allison. I will never feel a pressure while writing them that outweighs the enthusiasm to do it. Not even when *Bird Box* does well for Netflix and then reaches the *New York Times* bestseller list, not even when I will sit down to work on its sequel, *Malorie,* for Del Rey. Books for me will always be kept in that safe place. All ideas behind glass. And the bond between Allison and me will be one I check daily, leaving room, of course, for the colder seasons.

And here, Rose and Kenickie, these two so clearly at their end.

Kenickie is quiet. Rose is back in the kitchen. The re-made *Evil Dead* plays on the screen, and whether it's good or not doesn't matter right now. Does it ever?

Tonight is a night of fear. Not only the movies but the mirror held up by Kenickie and Rose. The possibility of heart's change.

But I don't believe mine will change. I don't want it to.

Writing. Filming. Dancing. Acting. Sculpting. Telling jokes on a stage. Art is no doubt my refuge, my cabin, the place where my army cot remains, where I sit on its edge and stare off into the robust imagination around me, allowing each idea to make its case, respecting even the worst one.

The novel: the place where I can be legendary, super, supernatural, *anything*. It's the most exciting place I know. There's a cape, a mask, inside the experience. Is there any greater sorrow than to imagine a man who has lost his way, who cannot remember the address to his own home, where his bed grows cold, where once he wrote?

Maybe the images on the screen have something to do with it. Maybe it's the fact this remake isn't as vibrant as the original. It's a bit more serious. Maybe that's why the lights are slowly dimming on my mood.

Or maybe it's that fuckin' word again:

Deserve.

And this warring within me in which, suddenly, I feel I don't "deserve" anything. But no, *yes . . . something.*

We are alive and our spirit is alive!

As the movie plays loud, I think: I'd wear all black to the funeral of a novelist's spirit. I imagine I'd cry that day, regardless of whether I knew one thing about the writer.

Because everything I've thought tonight, and every thought I've had, can only exist upon the foundation of that artistic spirit. None of these thoughts can be examined without it. And those who don't have it are spared ever fearing its loss.

I'd wear all black to the funeral of a novelist's ambition.

And would I recognize that ambition, even in death? Would I place my hand softly on your shoulder and whisper: *She wanted to tell stories.* I think I'd know what type of spirit it was by the reaction of the funeral-goers. I think I'd read it still in the static face of the novelist against the white lining of the box.

How close can a novelist stand to their dead spirit without being driven mad?

Because there was once a time when that spirit propelled the novelist in everything they did. Whether they knew it or not. That spirit said it was okay to sleep in halls and to travel across America without any money because what were riches compared to the spirit and what moneyed-music on earth could rival the swishing of paper and pen? The spirit of the novelist dances to the invisible drummer. And she knows it!

I would wear all black to the funeral of a novelist's motivation.

People used to call it "selling out," but nobody knows what that means anymore. Yet the artist knows at all times where they're coming from. And is it so terrible a thing to dip a toe into the commercial world? Is it any different from the Brill Building songwriters hammering out hits in their piano cubicles at dusk? No. But the novelist has their private scales of justice, their inner golden half-spheres, and what lies in one and what fills the other is known. And if they ever hang unbalanced, okay, but if they were to stay that way . . .

I gotta stop thinking of piecemeal death.

As the images of the new *Evil Dead* continue through my weed fog (the possessed woman in this is pretty awesome-looking, by the way; they did a good job with her), I'm finding all my musings of artistic funerals too dark to ponder. And so I try to move on. I ask Allison what she thinks of the movie. But Allison recognizes small talk coming from me the way a twin would.

And . . .

I can't do it. I can't stop.

I still hear the sobs and feel the rain of those funerals. Because it *is* my biggest fear. The loss of spirit, ambition, motivation. And while all things have their arcs, there are some things that ought to be allowed to live forever.

I imagine Professor Barclay presiding over these funerals.

A frock of green and white: *This crazy man EXPERI-ENCED!*

"I'm officially too high," Allison says. "I mistook the TV for a picture on the wall and I'm looking right at it."

We laugh. Because sometimes it's funny to get too high. And it's fun to lose control of a night. The movie has become a twirl of images, and I realize I'll never know what I think about this unless I see it again.

"It's really rather good," Kenickie says.

Rose (who I didn't realize was standing behind the couch), says: "Okay, Josh, one more question."

Kenickie doesn't stop her. It's like he's out of gas. Out of fighting words. I turn around to face her.

"Hit me," I say.

"But you must've known *Bird Box* was special as you wrote it," she says. "You've got a dozen novels and you said you didn't finish four others, and so I'm thinking, he knows the difference between good and bad, and *Bird Box* not only made the cut, and not only did you finish it but you also knew to send it to the agent when that time came. And then . . . it got picked up. She sold it for you. So . . . while you're talking so much about spirit over strategy, you had to know *Bird Box* would sell better, or else you woulda sent the agent something else."

Kenickie only eyes me. Maybe he wants to hear the answer too.

"The rough draft was written in twenty-six days," I say. "I didn't drink any of those nights. Not all rough drafts come so smooth. But at the same time, I don't know. *Wendy* generated so much heat, I could smell the draft. And *Goblin* was all I could talk about. *The Wolverine Line* was after a year off, and I think it's the book when I realized I was going to be doing this regularly forever. *Bring Me the Map* was the most meaningful, personally, up to the point when I wrote it. *Inspection* was almost an accident. And *Unbury Carol* took fifteen days. So, I mean . . . what I'm saying . . . I've felt something special about each of them."

"But why not *The Wolverine Line*? Why not shop that one?"

"I'm not sure. The rough draft was in crazy shape. Still is. Messy. And I love *Bird Box*. I love them all. I guess one of them had to be first, right? I just guessed right. But I don't know. Maybe we'd be talking about *The Wolverine Line* if I'd done that."

"I guess I just feel like you're not articulating the struggle of it," Rose says.

I think of the bookseller she mentioned again. Guppy. Is this what he didn't like about me? Did he wanna talk struggle and I came across Pollyannaish? I understand. A lot of people think struggle is the only truth.

Nobody ever says "He says it like it is" about an optimist.

That's telling . . .

"I like you, Rose," I say.

There's a funny beat of silence, and then we all laugh. Because it's a weird, high thing to have said. But I do. I like Rose for the way she talks, for the questions she has. For her presence that's bigger than the house.

Then . . .

"I once wrote the editor of a thesaurus he should be ashamed of himself for citing *idealism* as an antonym for *realism*," I tell them. "What are we teaching people if we're saying your ideal is the opposite of what's real? Mr. Laurence Urdang was more or less saying your dream is likely impossible. I bet he didn't think twice about using the words that way. He didn't respond to my letter, but I wanted him to. I wanted to sit down to lunch with the guy, get him to change that antonym for the next printing. Imagine a teenager, needing an antonym for realism . . . discovering idealism there . . ."

Rose slowly smiles. The light from the movie is flashing across her teeth.

We're all troubled. We're all navigating. We're all scared. But we're all brave too. We *do* work out our ideas and we *do* sit down to write. What for? Well, as Thax Douglas asked me in Chicago: *Isn't the act of writing itself optimistic?*

Next time someone says something nice, I'm gonna tell myself that person says it like it is. And I'm gonna try my best to mean it.

Even Laurence Urdang must've felt some propulsion, some spirit, when compiling the thesaurus, no?

"I'm not saying there's an ideal," I say. "I'm just saying it's not the opposite of real."

But when I look behind the couch again, Rose is gone.

"In love," Kenickie says, "one must be prepared to have their heart broken every day."

"It's gonna be all right," Allison says. "You're both amazing people."

He holds up a hand to say he's okay, he gets it.

"Even if it's just a moment's thought of a future sadness," he says. "You never wanna see the other person sad. Down. Mad. Your heart breaks a tiny bit every time you do. Because you want that ideal for them. All the time."

I think he's crying as he relaxes into the easy chair, but it's hard to tell as the light from the TV masks his face.

I realize he's comfortable now, being himself in full. The night has reached that point. The four of us have stepped through the introductions and small talk, the niceties and even the purpose for us getting together in the first place. It doesn't matter that we got together to watch a movie. The movie was brilliant, but the movie is over. Now we're each juggling our own thoughts, moods, worries, wants. But . . . publicly. Onstage. In front of one another. *For* one another. *We're* the movie now. Rose in the kitchen, Kenickie in the chair, me and Allison on the couch. The lighting in here is designed by the lighting on the screen. Dark, bright, quiet, loud. We're lit now by *Evil Dead,* and so, in the flashes, I see our individual moods: Rose's sad smile; Allison's bright, open eyes; Kenickie accepting what occurred tonight. He's making peace, onstage, live. Peace with the death of love. A former ideal, in the shape of young love, a onetime future that just didn't come to be.

"I'm glad you wrote that letter," he says to me, his eyes bright in the uneven shadows of *Evil Dead*. "Fuck Laurence Urdang."

IN THE COMPANY OF REALISTS

"I DON'T LONG FOR IDEAL," Allison says. "I just want *good*."

"Amen," Kenickie says.

"But," she says, "ideal can get us started. If I have a painting in mind, I'm seeing the ideal version. And I'll try to reach it. And for that, I paint."

"And are you sad if you don't reach it?" Kenickie asks. "And does this break Josh's heart?"

"No," she says. "Not sad. Because I'm able to think both things at once. The ideal and the fact there isn't one."

Brilliant. The doublethink of the artist. The necessary doublethink of the artist.

"I love that," I say. "On the one hand we wanna write this incredible book, on the other . . . the fact we're writing at all is ideal."

"And what's incredible? And to who?" Kenickie says. He points to the movie. "This is someone's favorite movie of all time."

We all look to the screen.

"Maybe that's why artists are crazy geniuses," Allison

says. "Because they have to hold these opposing truths. Maybe that's why we love artists so much. They hold them for us. Without them holding the ideal, we're all just in the company of realists."

The phrase is chilling.

I imagine a planet of realists. Not one dreamer on the street. All logic, all reason. I imagine a cartoonist telling himself he won't reach the ideal, so why bother? A dancer removing his shoes because . . .

Oy. I don't wanna have these thoughts.

But what Allison said . . .

And *dreamer* feels like the wrong word. We're awake, aren't we? We're punishingly awake. Yet the doublethink of the artist: for the dream is

. . . our

. . . body

. . . of

. . . work.

In our darkest moments, we have our body of work.

In our self-doubt, our body of work.

In despair and unreason, our body of work.

In heartbreak, our body of work.

In mistakes, in error, in regret, our body of work.

Not a crutch but a *place*. An ever-expanding place we go when we lose clarity.

The transcendentalist knows this as a place too. And what is a body of work if not proof of deliberate, consistent meditation? How many books have I written with my eyes rolled back into my head like the demons on the screen, the story rolling out before the whites of my eyes?

The invisible drummer drums. Listen! She plays our song. And the song goes . . .

All of us lurk, in our body of work.

Inspiration stands outside the office door, flat to the hall wall. He licks his lips; he thinks it's funny you have to wait for him. It turns the monster on. He will not enter the office for days, weeks, as you work, worry, fear. But one day you rise from the office chair, rise to the rhythm of your drummer, and you think . . .

I was born inspired.

And he knows you no longer need him. And so, scared now himself, he rushes into the office, groveling, on his knees, hands together, please forgive me, please forget all I've done, please let me stay!

LET ME INSPIRE!

And so, you sit down to write again. To the drummer's beat, you write. As Inspiration stands now in the corner of the office, scared to leave you now, scared to snicker. And you hold a singular truth in your head: *I no longer need him.*

And you ask Inspiration to knit this phrase in needlepoint so you can hang it on the office wall. And even he works to the rhythm of those drums.

Now . . . we write. Now . . . we transcend. Now we no longer compare or doubt or Vindicate or Validate or find Victory or Vengeance.

Now we add to the body of work.

[BEAT]

"*Farewell Chimeras*," I say. "That's a book title of Mark's. A book he wants to write. Or wanted to. The title has always haunted me. Does he mean goodbye to things that are unachievable? Meaning hello to things that are? Or does he mean a farewell to ideals? I like to think it's the former, but I don't know. Both are great. See, that's the thing . . ." I turn to face Kenickie, but he's gone now too. Where are they, Rose and Kenickie? The kitchen? Out back? Up the hall again, one more try?

"None of what we're talking about tonight means the work itself can't be the most pessimistic thing ever written," I say to Allison. "Bring that on. Please. Anything goes. Any take, any angle, any point of view. Some of my favorite books left me feeling hollow. Feeling terrible! It's the delivery that lifts you up, not necessarily the meaning or message itself. It's the fact the writer was able to pull this off, to convey, to transfer how they were feeling onto the page. I cry at the end of *Carrie* every time I watch it."

"That one makes you cry?" Allison says. "The prom scene?"

"Yeah. Amy Irving and that dude are beneath the stage. Carrie is on her way to receive the crown. And De Palma does this unbelievable slow pan up the rope, switching back and forth between all the characters, till we're up top with the bucket of pigs' blood. But it's not the emotion of the moment that gets me. It's not the fact Carrie White is about to be made a fool of or that she's going to lock the gym doors and blow the place up. It's how fuckin' good the scene is. De Palma pulls off at least one of those moments in every movie of his. Where I'm completely moved solely because of how *good* it is. So, tonight? All this talk of enthusiasm . . . we're not talking about writing about puppies and positivity. Jesus. I'm a horror lover. But behind the darkest works is the *desire* and energy to do the work in the first place. *That's* what makes me. *That's* what lifts me up. And sometimes, Allison, I even cry about my own stuff because maybe I know I wrote my way through a hard time, an anxious time, and when the period ended, when the anxiety finally lifted, I had left myself these . . . breadcrumbs. It's like leaving yourself a present. A map. A way out. Breadcrumbs on the path. If you get lost? Follow the crumbs back to the first song you ever wrote, the first story you ever tried to write. *That's* something to cry about. Because it's something good you did for yourself. And when people ask if you write for yourself or for an audience, I never know what to say. You start to see it as medicine. For the future you. No matter what's going on or how busy I am, I wanna make sure I work through that period, every period—that I get something new out of every phase of my life. Our life. It's a matter of keeping the breadcrumbs on the path."

"Creation as North Star."

"Yeah."

I think of the word *deserve* again. And without examining it, I feel fulfilled. The answer to the question is in there. I know it now.

We're quiet for a moment. Then we lean in and kiss. Allison feels like the personification of everything we've talked about tonight. She feels like the joy of writing, and never getting lost, and the doublethink of the ideal and the real.

We are optimists, always, in the company of realists.

"Josh."

It's Kenickie, calling to me from the kitchen.

"Yeah?"

"Wanna step outside a second?"

"Sure."

I get up and Allison pets Clip and I can't even focus on the screen anymore; it's all sepia colors and screams.

"Rose?" Allison calls behind me. "You in the bedroom?"

I hear a muffled yes, and I leave the living room and see Kenickie standing at the open back door.

"One more hit," he says. "For good luck."

I follow him out and we're standing by the garbage cans and the sky looks as vibrant as it is dark.

"We broke up just now," he says. "And that's a wrap on that."

"Ah, man."

"Yeah, well, I wanted to thank you guys for being cool about it. I mean, we literally broke up with you here. What a thing for company."

"Sorry, Kenickie."

"Yeah, but at the same time I think having you guys over made it easier or something. Sorry if we made a scene."

"Oh, don't worry. I write scenes all day."

He smiles.

"But I think what matters," he says, "is it's okay for two people to be wrong for each other. They can both still be pretty good on their own."

"You both are."

"And you dated the person for a reason, you know?"

"Yeah."

I'm thinking of my own breakups. Heartaches. And how with each one, no matter how awful they were, there was a distant sound of a door opening down the hall.

A new phase.

And I think about those breadcrumbs. And how they mark phases as much as they mark the path. I think how all my go-to artists went through distinct phases. A few books in a row or a few paintings in a row made up a period of their body of work. I think of the phrase *of a piece*. And I wanna call Mark and tell him we should write an album called *Of a Piece* and it wouldn't matter if the songs are of a piece or not; it's the phases that are.

"You got some balls," Kenickie says. "Weird ones, but balls nonetheless. A lot of dudes wouldn't talk about art like this. But I can feel it too. You know? And I know when you say *artist* you mean something else."

"Tell me more."

I'm hoping he words it in a way I will use for the rest of my life.

"I think when you say *artist* you mean *inventor*. I imagine you in a lab, a bunch of beakers bubbling over, giant machines steaming. I think of Igor waiting for the word to pull the lever. I think you're like Frank N. Stein after all. You're not looking to *capture the human condition,* you're looking to bring the story to life, my man."

I see a bat flutter across the sky. Two of them now. Love? Love between bats in the dark sky?

Kenickie goes on: "You're stitching all these parts together, right? Like you said. The parts of the body like the parts of a book, but you're stitching, like, all these books and songs and movies, too, all those body parts. And you're living the same life we are and you're dealing with your own shit. Your parents married?"

"No."

"Right. You said that. You got shit too. We all got shit. And you've got this . . . body of work. And that's the monster's body for you. But you don't need lightning. Your lightning is saying, Hey, we can do this, and hey, creating is good no matter if the creation is good or not." He pauses. Hits the joint. Hands it to me. I do the same. I think again: *Of a Piece.* "You ever wish your body of work could just get up and terrorize the town?" he asks.

"Fuck *yes,*" I say.

Then we laugh a little. 'Cause we're high and it's funny and Kenickie is experiencing heartbreak.

"I like writing in a field on the fringe," I say. "I like being a little freaky. I'll see people groaning how horror isn't taken seriously, or how it isn't up for an Oscar, and I'm thinking, Thank God. Let us be the creeps in the shadows."

"You like the look on people's faces when you tell them you write horror."

"I do."

We both watch bats in the sky. The joint's smoke rises toward them like fog from *The Evil Dead*.

"Hey, Kenickie. I think the hardest part of a breakup is that, at one point, you believed this was your forever reality. You saw a future with this woman. And maybe in the vision you grew old and maybe you had kids, and either way, a real future. And you believed that future. And so when things end, there's this sense that reality, or a potential reality, was yanked out from under you. Sometimes I think that's what we grieve when we grieve love. The fact that we believed something that didn't end up coming true. And then it's like . . . what else are we wrong about?"

"Yeah, well, I wasn't thinking kids."

We laugh again.

"You know," he says, "those movies are the perfect fuckin' movies to have watched tonight. It's like, kinda like what you're saying, I guess. These people head to a cabin, thinking they're about to have a fun little vacation, and then, splat, they're all demons and insane. And half the shit that scares Ash isn't the demon stuff but the fact that reality was yanked out from under him. You can see that in his eyes the whole time. Until *Army of Darkness* maybe. Then he's a badass. But he's not just battling demons, he's battling this . . . *change*."

Change. The unknown.

Again, I think of phases. Periods. And how the brave writers are the ones who do change, who do stretch, who acknowledge something more fundamental than routine. Because if who we are changes over time, shouldn't the stories we tell?

"We're gonna have to do this again with *Friday the 13th*," Kenickie says.

"We'll have to start earlier in the day," I say. "Fit in all fifty movies."

"Sounds so good."

"So good."

He smiles and steps toward me and suddenly we're hugging, and for a second I know Kenickie is crying into my chest and then, just as suddenly, we're looking up to the sky again, watching for the bats again, but no bats come.

Yes, periods. And what period are you in? And what period am I in? Over the years following the night we watch *The Evil Dead*, I'll write dozens more novels. And it won't be until I make a master list that I'll begin to see those periods clearly. Three books circling one theme, then three that circle another. But I'll notice, too, that each book is an answer to the one before it. *Bird Box* is bullet-tight, scant prose. It was followed by a kitchen-sink novel in *Bring Me the Map.* This pattern of reacting to my own stuff will continue for years, not unlike the periods of popular music, and how the youth will invariably rebel against the status quo. I think how every artist can be both. The old guard and the youth, so long as he or she rebels against what they did before, while always respecting each phase for what it was and what it is.

The back door opens. Allison comes outside.

"You guys smell like my grandmother's grasserole."

It takes a second for the joke to hit Kenickie and then he starts laughing, and then he can't stop. I smile Allison's way because she did something nice for him on a weird night.

She made him laugh.

"The movie's done," she says.

"Wow, really?" I ask.

And I sound sad, and so we all start laughing again because it's ridiculous to be sad that a movie is over, one we could simply rewind. At the same time, despite the darkness Kenickie and Rose must be enduring, it feels like this night should go longer. Should last forever.

Or at least long enough for me to answer the question that's been nagging me for days now.

What does an artist deserve?

"*Evil Dead 2*," I say.

"You're nuts," Kenickie says.

"You're never gonna remember it," Allison says.

She's right. I won't. None of us will.

But still . . . it feels like a lifeline. Like a way to buy a little more night.

"I'm in," Rose says.

Her voice comes from the back of the small yard, not the house. We all jump at the sound. She emerges from deep shadows created by the low-hanging branches of a red maple. Beyond her is the alley. A concrete path just wide enough for a single car. I remember walking that alley back when my friends and I wrecked the Blarney Stone pub. I can see our ghosts, the dozen of us, laughing and shouting, high-stepping our way from the bar, enough energy to power a city.

How long has Rose been standing there? Long enough to hear Kenickie's heartbreak?

"Then let's do it," Allison says. "Now or never."

Then suddenly there's a hand on my shoulder, and an exaggerated crawling toward my face.

It's Kenickie's.

"*Evil Dead 2,*" he says. "It's all about the hand."

"I don't know," Rose says. "I think it's more about the disintegration of relationships into demonhood."

THIN WINGS IN THE SKY

A THREE-MOVIE NIGHT IS PROBABLY ILL-ADVISED. Years later Allison and I will watch all five *Twilight* movies in one day with her sister Anna. But that was under the weight of an Upper Peninsula blizzard. Usually two movies or more means six drinks or more and once you get to three movies . . . chances are you could be watching *Air Bud* and not know the difference.

Still, they happen.

And, so, we're watching *Evil Dead 2*.

And it starts before I know it.

And, man, this title card. Already great.

We're back in the living room, but it's like we've all got frayed ends now. Allison and I aren't sitting prim on the couch. We're sprawled. Kenickie is on the edge of the easy chair, his head drops to his hands before popping up again. Rose stands up, sits again, stands, and sits.

"This is how the first one starts," Allison says. "Just less people."

It's true, Ash and Linda heading to the cabin. She's even

wearing a Michigan State shirt. She's wearing the necklace too.

"It's a remake," Rose says.

"It's not," Kenickie says. "It's a revamp of the start."

"Told from a different angle," Allison says. "Is this seriously how this goes?"

"Isn't it great?" I say. "Who would think to do this? To tell the same story in a different way in part two?"

He just found the tape recorder. All this in the first five minutes. As if Sam Raimi is saying, *Hey, we loved the demon-fighting scenes too. Wanna get right to 'em?*

He's even saying, *We don't need a reason here. A couple goes to the cabin. Forget part one. Here's a different version of the same events, with Ash as the constant in our experiment.*

Seriously, though, has this approach ever been taken before? This is no sequel. It's no wonder some people mistake this one for the first. In a way, it is.

"It is absolutely a remake," Rose says. "They remade their own movie. I love it. But it's true."

"You're wrong," Kenickie says.

Meanwhile, Linda's already a demon. And we all just witnessed the single greatest beheading in the history of cinema.

I ask Kenickie to rewind it because it's just that stylish, that good.

He does. We cheer.

Now we're seeing the same track shot that ended *The Evil Dead*. Through the cabin, up to Ash screaming.

"And so," Allison says, "those first five minutes were like a recap of the original."

"That's right," Kenickie says. "And so now we're continuing from where part one left off."

"But those first five minutes *aren't* a recap," Rose says.

"Not a literal one," Allison says. "But . . . mostly?"

I've never seen anything like it. What an idea. It would be like me writing a sequel to *Bird Box* in which the first ten pages feature Malorie and one kid (not two) leaving the house, heading up a river, getting where she got at the end of the book. Then, all new stuff from there. The question Sam Raimi must've asked himself is . . . Does it matter *how* Ash got here? Let's start with him here, now. Let's get to it.

But it's even more creative than that. Because it doesn't feel like Sam Raimi is thumbing his nose at his own first feature. I just know he's not. What he's doing is saying, Hello viewers, hello fellow filmmakers, *this* is what matters. So why not get to what matters?

"Whoa!" Rose says. She sits. She stands.

Because Ash just turned into a demon in a puddle.

"Jesus, this must've been fun to make," I say.

"A lot of work," Allison says.

Yeah, a lot of work. Fun work.

A variety of doublethink in itself.

I'm thinking about that now as the movie plays through

a wall of marijuana and magic. I look over and Kenickie is back in the kitchen, refilling drinks. I'm thinking of fun. *Merry.* As the demon wails rise from the TV, adventurous music to boot, I'm remembering this party in New York City back when the High Strung lived there. Mark and I are on the couch and we're talking about all the songs and all the books we want so badly to one day write. Before then, in college, we talked a lot about novels. It's one of our bonds: a songwriting duo, yes, but both with a drive to write novels. We'd tried, in our own ways, by the night of this New York City party. And a guy in denim doesn't like our enthusiasm.

We know him. Raoul's a little more New York than we are. He's spent more time here. And he's sure as shit doing better than we are financially. But this will be true of anyone we meet for at least the next ten years.

"You're going to burn out," Raoul tells me.

As a horror fan, I can't help but think the word *harbinger.* Here's the old man at the gas station telling us not to mess around on Smith Farm because blah blah blah.

"Me?" I ask.

I'm smiling because I'm polite. Maybe. Or maybe it hasn't fully registered that Raoul is the first person in my life who's telling me to slow down, possibly even to bow out of the life of the artist. A thing not even my parents will ever come close to doing, despite my being broke for more than a decade to come.

"You're moving too fast," Raoul says. "You've got a hundred ideas and you're making albums a mile a minute."

"Well, that doesn't sound so bad," I say.

I hadn't really considered the pace before this. A side of me wishes he hadn't pointed it out.

"I give you a year," he says. "Then you'll give up."

And he walks away and I stand up, I actually stand up with a mind to grab this guy by the denim collar, drag him back. Maybe I should've done that.

"What a dick," Mark says.

If there's one thing I'd never, *ever* do, it's discourage someone who's on a roll. I mean, okay, that can depend on the type of roll. But writing songs is a lot healthier than cocaine. Or . . . okay, maybe Mark and I *did* move too fast, and maybe we still do. Maybe we make too many albums and maybe one day I'll write too many books and a fella like Raoul won't know what to make of that. Maybe someone like him won't trust someone like me.

Years after the Night of Raoul, social-media platforms will become a very big deal. I'll see people discouraging others all the time in so many different ways. It'll become the kind of place where some people get mad if you post something, anything, positive. Most people wouldn't believe you if you posted how happy you are to be there. And I'll deal with that my own way (a documentary, a nonfiction book, for starters; an arena of my own), but on the Night of Raoul I had never encountered anything like it before. Yet somehow I didn't freak out on the guy.

But just because you don't air your grievances, it doesn't mean you don't have any.

The Night of Raoul is the night I discovered the Four V's, for myself, as Raoul drank with others (presumably people who moved slower), and Mark and I resumed our conversation, ideas for the next group of songs. Years later, while watching *Evil Dead 2* with the woman of my fantasies (beyond my fantasies: nobody could've imagined Allison), I will get up and go to the bathroom and I'll be just high enough to stand before the bathroom mirror and say: "I didn't slow down, Raoul. If I seemed wide-eyed to you, it's because I was. If I appeared naïve or uninformed, it's because I was. If I appeared to be moving a hundred miles a minute, it's because I was."

I feel like I'm back at that loft party. The toilet-paper roll to my right looks like it's made of denim.

"But don't give up, Raoul. On whatever you're doing. Don't quit on your dreams just because someone told you there's a right pace and a wrong pace to these things. It's your pace, Raoul. Whatever you want that to be. However fast. However slow. And I hope you've found that rhythm, I hope you hear your drummer."

I pause here. I nod. This is what I want to say to Raoul.

I turn from the mirror. I slap my face. Trying to get rid

of this serious expression before heading back to the third movie of the night.

But I haven't left New York yet . . .

Out there, straight from college, Mark and I decided to read a lot of the books we hadn't read at Michigan State. Books we were assigned but were too busy starting a band to read. These were blisteringly bright days. Blank pages felt like hallways, staircases, buildings, cities we'd never been to. We already had two totally important things going for us: the unfounded confidence to set out and the horror of failing to try. But in those days, the former outweighed the latter by so much, the fears could almost be funny. We read constantly. Spent so much time in New York City bookstores. Mark even worked at the Strand. One night, the power in our weird little apartment went out and we read Hemingway out loud by candlelight.

These were *burning* bright days. We'd already moved to New York, yes, and we'd already experienced our bandmates leaving East Lansing before we'd graduated, yes, and we'd reacted well to that exodus, buying a 4-track machine to record our own albums rather than packing it in. We'd already passed so many tests, seen so many peers give up on the life, even as we doubted ourselves and regained our footing. Nothing could be quite like those early days in New York City, surrounded by so much bustle, business, ambition, goals, people, romantic possibility, music, drugs, booze, fear, and fire. Mark got mugged a few times out there. I walked at night with my keys in my clenched fist like little Freddy Krueger knives. We were told by locals never to mess in anybody else's business. We heard horror stories of people who had. One night I saw, two blocks ahead, a woman jumped by three men who had been hiding behind a parked van. I reached for the pay phone beside me, but the woman kicked one guy and swung her purse at another, and the three attackers darted before I could call 911. Close call. For all. I befriended a heroin addict out there, brought her to the High Strung's loft, where we all lived, which she said was grosser than any heroin den she'd ever seen. She told me her ex-boyfriend had stabbed a man with a needle on the subway, a man he suspected of being involved with her. One afternoon he entered the bar we were drinking at. He didn't stab me.

The High Strung saw the Twin Towers fall in New York City. In person. We watched them fall.

What scenes, these, memories played out on the biggest American stage. A dome of storming emotions and (sometimes) dangerous turns, all an endless gale above me and Mark, the two of us huddled beneath, talking plans, goals, *what we could do,* in our own tiny pocket of that juggernaut's sandbox. We wrote lyrics and outlines on the apartment walls, recorded until sunup on a reel-to-reel machine in my bedroom. A machine not unlike the one Ash listens to in *The Evil Dead.*

These were radiant, fearful days.

What is young love, and where does it fit on an arc without end? Did the arc start in New York City? East Lansing? In our respective childhood homes, where I in mine stood before my parents and read for them an entire children's book from beginning to end? Then later, *Bunnicula, Howliday Inn,* and *The Celery Stalks at Midnight*? And where Mark, in his, listened to Bob Dylan's *Biograph* alone in his bedroom, nobody to talk to about the infinity he'd heard in the lyrics? Did it begin when we started the band, the two of us co-songwriters and singers, a team that will still be writing together twenty-five years later?

On the screen in Rose and Kenickie's house: Sam Raimi and Bruce Campbell at work, at play. Their early days. And I'm thinking early days. There were times I scared myself, feared how *badly* I wanted to finish a novel. Like I could go legally crazy if I didn't. I "failed" at four of them. *George Wax: Man of Wax* was a favorite of the unfinished books. I was frustrated, I was trying. The girl I was dating at the time told me I couldn't be like Jack Kerouac, couldn't just squeeze a novel out like that. I got mad when she said it, drove the novel to a gas station, tossed it in the garbage by the pump. The thing had been written on a typewriter. I'd never see it again. Except, later that night I went after it.

I had to have it. Finished or not.

It sits in a crate in my office to this day. Adding, always, every day, to the momentum, the process of *writing*.

Then, years on the road, Mark leaves the band. Despondent, feeling alone, I try a fifth novel. I think I'll write two at once. When I get stuck on one, I'll turn to the other. The first is about a young man shoveling snow for an eccentric local, eavesdropping on that local's enviable life. The second is a psychosexual horror story set in the woods outside a fictional Michigan town. I made it two pages into the former, turned to the latter, and . . .

"Exploded," I say in Rose and Kenickie's living room.

"What?" Allison says.

"I just exploded through *Wendy*. I didn't take a day off for twenty-eight days, and when I saw the ending was gonna happen, that I was going to *finish a book,* I leapt out of the coffee shop chair. This was at four A.M., in a twenty-four-hour place. Sometimes I feel like I'm still in that moment. I'm still there. The excitement of seeing that ending hasn't faded yet."

Allison is smiling but nodding the way people do when they're thinking: *What?*

"You're high," Rose says.

"Tell that bookseller Guppy to fuck himself," I say.

And the three of them break into laughter, and even I start laughing, thinking of those days, the days that all led to this one, here, now, living the life in full, unconsciously committed, just as in love now as then, just as scared now as then.

It's all one young love, the night we watch *The Evil Dead.*

Meanwhile, Ash just chainsawed his demon girlfriend's head down the middle.

Ash in the mirror now.

"There's a ton of Charlie Chaplin to this movie," Allison says. "A direct line from silent films to these movies."

"They deserved everything they got," Kenickie says.

At first, I think he means the people who died at the hands of the demons or maybe the demons themselves.

But no. Kenickie's talking about Sam Raimi becoming successful.

That word. As if groaned by the demons themselves.

Deserve.

I imagine Kenickie standing outside my inner door. He's wearing an overcoat in the fog. He knocks.

(Ash chops off his own hand; the color of the blood on the screen is the best blood color I've ever seen.)

(*Who's laughing now?*)

It certainly still sounds dangerous to me, that word: *deserve*. If I start thinking I deserve success, awards, followers, likes, accolades, fame . . . what will happen to me? Will I become an asshole? Raoul was an asshole with none of those things. Could this happen to me?

"Well, they definitely deserved to make this movie," I say.

Something clicks inside me. A boxing bell goes off. Like in that big scene from Charlie Chaplin's *City Lights*. But I don't quite recognize it yet.

"What do you mean?" Rose asks.

"Well, I'm not sure what anything means anymore," I say. "But you can see how much work they put into this.

How much time, how many decisions. I don't know if anybody deserves anything exactly, but these guys deserved to make this movie."

That bell again. *Ding.* And I see Charlie Chaplin dance-stepping his way into the ring, hiding behind the referee.

Meanwhile, on the screen: the most amazing sequence with the laughing lamp as Ash loses his mind.

"But don't you think they deserve the success they found with it?" Rose asks.

Coming out of her mouth, the question sounds different from how it did in my head.

"Well, I guess if there's success to be had for making movies, then . . . I'm sorry. I don't know what I think about this yet."

She laughs. "Well, there is success to be had."

"Are you scared of success?" Kenickie asks.

"No," I say. "Well, I guess I don't know. Maybe. Are you? Maybe I am. I'm for sure scared of thinking I deserve anything. I wrote for so long without getting anything back. I loved every second of it."

"But you can't go through your whole career thinking you don't deserve anything either," Rose says. "You'll miss out on tons of opportunities that way."

I stand up. Charged by Jack and grass.

"That word freaks me out too," I say. "*Opportunities.* I don't want these words anywhere near what I'm doing. I get what you're saying, Rose. And it sounds so right coming from you, right now. But deserve . . . I deserve good ideas. Right? Don't I? Don't we all?"

"But you don't deserve readers?" Rose asks.

I'm thinking . . . thinking . . .

Readers, reviews, awards . . .

These words sound insane to me. Rantings.

"No, I don't," I tell her. "Or . . . I don't know. I haven't worked this out yet."

"Worked it out?" Rose asks.

"I feel like any answer I give right now would be a rough draft. I need time with this."

"There you go," Kenickie says. "Very writerly."

"There's a difference between *deserved* and *earned*," Allison says. "A person has earned the right to feel proud of what they do, so long as they put in the work."

"But not just the work," I say. "It's gotta be the right kind of work, right? It's gotta be the *core* work. What are we all really after here? I don't know . . ."

I'm anxious. Pacing in their living room. Too high.

Then the others get up too and we're all standing now. All four of us.

"Right," Allison says, "but when people say you deserve success, it's an innocent thing to say."

"Bingo," Kenickie says.

"They mean you worked hard and you're great and all that," Rose says.

"Great," I say. "But when you're alone with the writing . . . the books, and you turn the word . . . *deserve* . . . so that it's facing yourself . . . I just think it's better facing the window."

I'm trying to be funny. It's not landing. I'm nervous. Starting to freak out a little.

"It's dangerous, maybe," Allison says. "I can see that."

"But maybe also fuck that?" Kenickie says. "Why is it bad to think you deserve things? We don't have to be monks about it."

"You deserve water," Rose says. "Food, shelter, love."

"But there's something about the word," Allison says. "And if you deserve it, doesn't everyone?"

There's an answer to this question that's been eluding me for days. I can feel it's close. In the room with us. Bathed in the light of *Evil Dead 2*.

"But what if someone just isn't as good as you are?" Kenickie asks. "Say there's a guy who writes as much as you do, he's got, like, a hundred novels, but they just aren't as good."

"That guy sounds incredible," I say. "I'd love to watch *Nightmare on Elm Street* with him."

"You're avoiding the subject," Rose says. "You *are* scared of success, aren't you?"

"Let's not talk about me," I say. "Let's talk about . . . Frank N. Stein."

"I'd read every book by Frank N. Stein," Kenickie says. "And you'd spoil them for me, Rose."

I move fast here: "So, Frank writes no matter where he

is, no matter how much time is already spoken for. Because if you wanna be an artist, you *have* to finish works of art. And if you wanna be a writer . . . well. He *finds* the time to get it done, even if it's a few minutes every other day. He fights through all his own mental anguish; he rides the cliché roller coaster of thinking his own work is brilliant, then loathing it. All that. He puts his heart into every book, and he knows he does because that's the kind of thing you just know. He's very much alive. This Frank N. Stein."

"*ALIVE!*" Rose says.

"*IT'S ALIVE!*" Kenickie says.

They laugh, together. I almost pause. To give them this moment. But I don't think either of them wants it.

"What does Frank deserve?" I ask.

"He deserves it all, man," Kenickie says. "Sellin' books. Movies made. All of it. If he worked his ass off *and* his shit is good? If he doesn't deserve it, who does? *Based on the book by Frank N. Stein.*"

"If he's scared of success," Rose says, "maybe he deserves a quiet life of reading."

"That's interesting," I say. "So, you think Frank deserves the life he wants to lead?"

"Well, yeah, we all do."

"Right. Allison?"

"Thinking," she says.

Even as Ash bangs on the cellar like a madman.

I'll swallow your soul!

Rose says, "What about people who put their all into just getting attention? Do they deserve that then?"

"I don't think that's what he's saying," Kenickie says.

But Rose goes on: "And what if someone sets out with only money on their mind and they put all their energy into *that*?" Rose says. "It sounds fuckin' awful for someone like that to actually get it."

"Okay, then it's a combination," Allison says. "A mix of intent and the medium. What an artist deserves is totally different than what an athlete deserves."

"Or a mathematician," I say.

"Yep," she says. "If you're playing with numbers, you get straight answers."

On the screen, Ted Raimi just played a demon. Years later I will go see a friend's DJ set at a restaurant only a few doors down from the building where the *Evil Dead* guys had their office. Ted Raimi will also know this friend. We will be the only two there to catch the set. We will sit together at a table and talk about our mutual friend. I will think of the night Allison and I watched *The Evil Dead* when we do.

"Nobody can *deserve* a good reaction," Allison says.

"Right," I say.

"Why not?" Kenickie asks.

Allison's pacing now too.

"And he can't *deserve* the bestseller list," Allison says.

"Right."

"And he can't *deserve* people to understand him, what he's done."

"Right."

"So how the fuck will he know if it's good?" Rose asks.

"Because an artist knows when they did something good," Kenickie says.

"How would you know that?"

"I mean, come on," Kenickie says. "Am I right, guys?"

I think of Allison's paintings, the way she plays classical guitar, her singing voice.

"Yes," we both say at the same time.

"But only good in and of itself," Allison says.

"But how can someone be expected to hang on to that," Rose asks, "if literally nobody ever tells them it's good?"

"That's why Frank N. Stein writes so many books," I say. "Because he hasn't worked that out yet. He doesn't even think of that yet."

"He just moves," Allison says. Then she dances a little to the music from the movie.

But is this true? None of it feels definitive. None of it feels like an answer to the question.

"He should never in a million years sell himself short on how many good things might come from his books," I say. "But he's gotta at least know the meaning of the word *deserve*. Or else that word is going to ruin him. He's gonna compare himself to others because everybody's in the same game . . . but only Frank can write Frank's books.

Right? Man, it's gonna be a dark place he goes every time he sits down to write if he's thinking about . . . *deserve*."

"Ah," Rose says. "So, there's what you deserve to feel and what you deserve to get."

"I still think you deserve to get everything anybody else does," Kenickie says.

"But then, what's good and what's bad, right?" I say. But I don't wanna go down this road. Because this isn't really what I'm talking about. There's gotta be someone who doesn't like the movies we've watched tonight. As impossible as that sounds.

I take a deep breath. The others are waiting for me to say something, but there's a lot of blood on the screen.

"Maybe you deserve to find something of yourself in what you do," I say.

But this sounds tired. And no more definitive.

"Finding your identity by way of what you write can be a dangerous thing too," Rose says.

"But Josh likes that idea," Allison says.

"I do. I think . . ."

"I keep hearing that," Rose says.

I'm pacing. Breathing deep.

"But imagine you've had this novel idea for years," I say. "You finally write it, somehow, anyway. Really try to picture the stack of pages, the story, the characters and scenes you dreamed in all those dreaming days. And now, it's fuckin' done. There's a sense of identity in having done what you set out to do. You can count on yourself that way. You are the kind of person who does what he sets out to do. The book is proof. And there's *identity* in that."

"Except paying the bills is nice too," Rose says.

"I'm just trying to think of an equal to this," I say. "Outside of art."

"Love." Of all the people in the room, Kenickie says it.

Rose scoffs. But maybe I hear a kinship there. Just because their love is dying doesn't mean they don't remember believing in it.

"Okay," I say. "Okay, yeah. We see ourselves in those we love, and they see themselves in us."

I snap my fingers just as a snapping sound comes from the TV, and here I am standing in Allison's cousin's living room, high and drunk, *Evil Dead 2* on the screen, and I suddenly feel completely in tune.

"By finishing a story," I say, "by raising it from the dead, right . . . you get *next* to it. Like a lover." I'm moving faster now, can't stop. "Every idea for a book is a ghost, right? Or like the pieces of the body Frankenstein's gotta collect to put the thing together. So, you got the unmatched pieces, the brain, the heart, and of course Frankenstein's *desire* to do this in the first place. All the body parts are the parts of your book idea. All strange and unmatched. A big left hand, a smaller right. You don't even know what you *need,* but you know it's gotta speak in the end. Or at least walk. And the electricity . . ."

Thinking . . .

"The electricity is the process," Allison says. "Because that's the moment it goes from dead to alive."

"Well, that's good," Rose says.

"Great!" I say. "You've got the pieces stitched together, and now the electricity to bring the thing to life. Then, once the book sits up? Oh my God. There you are. You're next to it. And there's your answer, Rose. Just like I wanna be near Allison. And I wanna be near friends. And I go to parties because I wanna be near the *energy* there. Anything can happen once the book sits up! Frankenstein could change the path of modern medicine, but will any moment ever be any bigger for the doctor than when the monster opens its eyes?"

"But aren't you a victim if you don't achieve success?" Rose asks.

We all look at her. What does this mean?

"Think about it: You put all your heart and soul into a thing, and it turns out to be a kickass book. But then . . . nothing comes of it. Why didn't anything come of it? And aren't you a victim of the people who thought you couldn't make it? The people who don't think you're any good? The people who maybe don't like you because of who you are rather than what you're writing? How does that fit into all this? How can someone be the victim and a success story at the same time?"

"Well, let me speak for me," I say. "And I'm neither one of those things. No matter what's come before, and no matter what comes next, I'm neither a victim nor a success. I've discovered, for myself, in my life, the joy in creation. The doctor. Who cares who laughs at the doctor? Who cares who doubted him? He's fulfilled."

"Rare as roofing supplies arriving on time," Kenickie says. "And fuck yes to everything you're saying now."

"I think one of the reasons people are so upset in the world is because they don't have anywhere to express themselves," I say. "If you have an outlet, if you believe you're represented, even piecemeal, by what you do in your daily life . . . if you are *expressed* throughout the day . . . you won't feel as desperate to declare yourself, all of you, say, online. I'm neither a victim nor a success, because one is the past and one is the future and when I'm writing and when I'm talking about writing, I'm *here*."

"Writers play the victim all the time," Rose says. "They claim people told them they sucked. All that."

"How many people?" I ask. "One person? Two? One jerk at a party in New York City? Another, an old friend, who came to say you needed a plan B? Is this the discouraging armada? To take someone's opinion seriously, they'd have to know everything about us. Who we are, what we're planning, what we're capable of. But nobody can know this. Literally nobody. So, anybody who ever told you to stop writing was talking to someone else."

"Amen," Allison says.

"Maybe if hundreds of thousands of people told you to stop, I'd feel for you," I say. "But who doesn't have one or two jerks in their lives? This guy in New York . . . he tells me I'm gonna burn out. He says it like he knows it. This is before I've written one book." Again, years from that night, I'll be working on my thirty-eighth. It will be this work, different from anything else I've done, a nonfiction account of my night with Allison and *The Evil Dead*. "Who was he talking to? Who does he know?"

"He was talking to himself," Rose says.

"Maybe," I say. "But I think he was talking to a cliché. An idea of a life or dreams. I don't know what led him to that moment, and while I could feel sympathy for his worldview . . . I don't have the steam for that tonight. *Tonight* . . . I'm thinking there is no budget for writing a book. And there is nobody who you know with enough power to get you to write a classic of the genre. Years after they made *The Evil Dead*, Stephen King wrote an article for *Twilight Zone: Magazine* saying someone's got to put this movie out. He'd seen it at a festival. And so someone did. But they'd already made a classic, with or without his help. You see what I'm saying? Did they deserve the distribution?"

"We deserved to see it," Rose says.

"That's not what he means," Kenickie says.

"Well, what do you mean?" Rose says. "Because the way I see it, if you're going to be interviewed on panels and podcasts, then you better have this shit lined up, ready to talk about."

"I'm trying," I say. "But what am I . . . a philosopher? A

fashion designer? A model? An influencer? Why do people value these things in their writers? I just want to be a writer. Nothing bigger, but nothing smaller too."

"But books are just as curated as anything else," Rose says.

"No," I say. "And that's what I love about fiction: It doesn't lie about what it is. There's no pretending to be anything other than a story. And any meaning anybody finds in *Bird Box,* well, it may be what I had in mind, it may not. But either way, there's nothing strategic about the books. Just like there's nothing strategic about my relationships with my friends, my family, with Allison. I'm running on instincts at all times. Just like you are. I have total respect for the books. And the moment I start saying I deserve anything more than them is the moment I start seeing them as less than the reward they are."

That bell again. Loud as hell now. Inside me. I'm close to explaining this. For myself. I'm close to articulating an answer to the question that has been haunting me.

I think of Professor Barclay in front of the class, going on and on, a serpentine lecture. And no matter how confusing or meandering he got, by the end of it you understood.

"I miss the days when all we knew about writers was a single author photo, and sometimes not even that," Rose says. "Just a name. And even that I didn't always read."

We all look to the screen. We've hardly been watching *Evil Dead 2.* We've been standing, pacing, talking. I start understanding this night is legendary, in its own weird way. And that *The Evil Dead* sparked the whole thing.

"Shots," I say. Which is a bad idea. I know it is. Between the grass, the energy, the movies, if I start doing shots I'm gonna black out.

But it doesn't take more than that one syllable for Kenickie to be up; for Rose to be saying, Hey, hey, no way; for Allison to be asking me if this is a good idea. She's seen the hangovers firsthand. But we're talking about the nature of art, of success, and I'm scared of what's to come no matter what comes and I'm so excited, too, so unbelievably excited about what's to come.

As we head to the kitchen, it strikes me.

Aren't I already living a life of letters? Hasn't what's coming already come? How is the hallway I lived in for a year, the basements, the flophouses, the short bus circling the country, how are the growing stacks of rough drafts, new processes, new approaches to each book, how are the late nights of electrifying talks and roller-coaster drinks, how are the thoughts, the feelings, the passions, the purities, the horrors, the lack of finances, the just-getting-by, the falling in love with every friend, boy or girl, the dreams the nightmares the writing, the writing, freehand, the writing, a typewriter, a guitar, the writing, a laptop, one book two books three books thirteen, how is this blindingly brilliant party of a profound life any less than the life of letters lived by every writer who's ever written before?

I'm walking toward the kitchen with my stack of rough drafts walking beside me. I *am* living a life of letters! And I have been! I started living it before New York City, but it was the ten years of "failing" when I was let into the club, when the doorman nodded and said, *This fuckin' guy is gonna try his fifth book after throwing the first four in wastebaskets across America. This is a man of letters.*

"Shots," Kenickie says. "I prefer your lady's tequila to your Jack."

"Never mix, never worry," I say.

But we're about to mix. So, a little worried.

Nobody hit Pause this time, and *Evil Dead 2* continues in the other room.

We do a shot. And because it's Kenickie, we do a second.

"We deserve these," he says.

"You don't deserve me!" Rose yells from the living room.

Kenickie leans in: "No, I've done nothing to deserve her."

We laugh.

"That's some interesting shit," he says. "It's good to know the writer I know actually cares about these things."

"Same to you," I say, hardly able to talk for the tequila. "It feels like we're standing on a vortex, doesn't it? That we're having this conversation at a meaningful moment in time?"

"They're all meaningful."

"They are."

So he pours two more shots. To the meaningfulness of all of time.

"Do you think this 'deserve' shit has anything to do with imposter syndrome?" Kenickie asks.

"What's that?" I ask.

Allison and Rose appear in the doorway.

"You two are going to regret whatever this is," Rose says.

"I want one," Allison says.

Kenickie lines her up a shot.

"Well, fuck you too," Rose says.

She fixes one for herself.

It strikes me people often gather in kitchens at parties. Why do all parties end up in the kitchen, whether people are eating or not?

"So, I've got an idea," Rose says. "Rather than *Army of Darkness* . . ."

They're all talking, but I'm sinking into thoughts about *imposter syndrome*. This is the first I've heard the phrase. I can guess what it means. It's the antithesis of everything I've learned.

Imposter syndrome.

It's the worst phrase I've ever heard.

Consider: I'm ten years old, riding shotgun as my dad drives at night. Someone is singing on the radio. The radio glows blue in the dark dashboard. Dad says, Damn, he always wished he could sing songs. I ask what does he mean?

Is there something Dad *can't* do? He smiles, says, Josh, this isn't like that. Some people are born for this. Some aren't. Right, I say, but you wanted to sing songs? And you . . . didn't? Did you try? Now he's not smiling so much, and I feel bad about that. That's not what I mean, he says. He says, again, Some people are made for it, some aren't. And I'm sinking into the big '80s passenger seat, hearing for the first time there's something Dad cannot do. Worse than that, though . . .

Something he wanted to do but did not try.

Imposter syndrome.

Before you even get started.

My first view of it, at ten.

Dad, are you not as quippy as Oscar Wilde? But neither was Edgar Allan Poe. So, are you not as frantic as Edgar Allan Poe? But neither was Virginia Woolf. Are you not as troubled as Virginia Woolf? But neither is Paul McCartney. Are you not as fluid as Paul McCartney? But neither was Dee Dee Ramone. Are you not as punk as Dee Dee Ramone? But neither was Charles Dickens. Are you not as traditionally skilled as Charles Dickens? But you hate traditionally skilled. Are you not as Southern as Faulkner? Bilingual as Nabokov? Poetic as Toni Morrison, or even Jim Morrison? But don't you see? None of these people had what another had. And each had their own way with words.

If you don't belong, who does?

"What do you think, Josh?" Rose asks me. "You're the

deciding vote. I'm for it, Kenickie is against it, of course. And Allison doesn't care."

Imposter syndrome. I'm thinking there are young writers in this world who worry they don't belong because their heroes are made of different stuff.

"*Josh,*" Rose says.

I look up. "What? What is it?"

They're all waiting for an answer. Allison is smiling. She makes the room brighter, every room I've ever been in.

"Rose wants to know if you wanna watch *Army of Darkness,*" Kenickie says.

But I recognize the night is much closer to the end than it is to the beginning.

"It's okay if we sleep here?" I ask Kenickie.

"I'd be seriously worried if you didn't."

I'm thinking he might need the couch. But he beats me to that punch.

"You two take the couch. I'll figure out what the hell I'm gonna do."

"So, no fourth movie," Rose says.

"That'll be our sequel," I say. "Watching *Army of Darkness.* And thanks for having us, Rose."

"Of course. It was awesome," she says.

The two of them walk up the hall. Kenickie looks back and gives me an okay sign before vanishing into the darkness. We hear doors close. Beds creak.

Allison and I are alone. It all feels so sudden. One of them must've taken Clip back with them. When did *Evil*

Dead 2 end? When did we leave the kitchen and return to the couch?

"Wow," Allison says. "This was a night to remember. I just hope we do."

But the night isn't over. Not quite. I feel like I've come up short on a quest. A faceless man stood in the fog and knocked on my inner door and asked:

What does an artist deserve?

And I haven't answered him yet.

"Hey, wait . . ." I say.

The house is end-of-the-night quiet. So sudden.

"What's up?" she says.

Did I get too high?

"I don't know," I say. "I'm anxious."

"Well, yeah."

I can't even pretend to smile. I'm feeling a little closed in. No, quite a bit.

"Come outside with me," I say.

"Sure."

"There are bats in the sky. Let's go outside."

To my anxiety, this sounds like a very good reason to step outside. Never mind the fact I'm feeling claustrophobic. Forget the fact I'm feeling suddenly hot, cold, hot again.

Bats.

I hurry through the kitchen, out the back door. Allison follows.

"Big night for them," she says.

"And we had no idea," I say.

But my heart's not in this conversation. I pace on the cement. I'm searching for how to feel comfortable inside. But it never works that way.

Years later, Allison will have suggestions to help with these anxiety attacks. They will work. But that's years later.

"Mark and I used to send copies of our cassette albums to a list of twenty people," I say. "That was enough. Now I'm thinking of all the ways *Bird Box* could go."

"I hear ya. But don't beat yourself up for it either. It's your first published book. Man, that's big."

I'm pacing. She's looking to the sky.

"Bat," she says. "Look."

I look but I'm either too late or my mind's eye is seeing so much other stuff, I miss it.

"Deserve," I say.

"Ah, you're still going for it."

"Yeah. I wanna answer this. Not just for tonight, but for . . . forever."

"All right, well, where are we at with it?"

I pace. "I don't know exactly."

"Well, inside the house you said they deserved to make that movie. That's a start."

I pace some more. I look her in the eye, her face lit by the porch light above the garbage cans. "I'm scared, Allison."

"I know you are."

We're quiet a beat. I hear thin wings in the sky. I mistake them for thoughts.

"About the future. About *Bird Box* and Kristin. All of it."

"I know. I get it. It's intense. You're putting yourself out there. You said it yourself, there's no medium as naked as the book."

"But . . . but that's *doublethink* . . . I'm also not scared."

"Bravery and fear aren't opposites," she says. "One literally comes after the other."

I pause, look her in the eye. Now I do smile a little. Because that was good.

"Okay, so . . ." I say.

Thinking. Pacing.

Inside, you said they deserved to make that movie . . .

"Do I deserve the book deal I got?"

"Of course."

"Right. But also . . . do I?"

She's thinking too.

"I can't think of a scenario in which you don't," she says.

"Does anybody who writes a book deserve a book deal?"

"Sure. If someone who can give them one likes it."

"Right. Okay. Well . . ."

We're quiet another beat. Up the street, loud voices exiting the Blarney Stone.

"Are you actually doubting whether or not you deserve it?" she asks.

"No."

"Then you're trying to . . ."

"Trying to articulate what matters."

But she knows this. We both do. In a way, it's what we always do.

. . . you said they deserved to make that movie . . .

But before I can ask myself why this phrase keeps returning, why it fascinates me, a young couple walks up the alley behind Rose and Kenickie's house. It's a man and a woman. Allison and I are so quiet they don't know we're here.

"We shoulda beat them," the man says.

"We almost did!"

"I know, Shelly. But come on! We had them."

"It's pool. You win some, you lose a lot of them."

"Okay, but . . . that one was ours."

I feel like I'm standing in front of the future. All of it. It's overwhelming. The possibilities. The different ways all this can go. I've never given much thought to the future. I've ignored strategy and planning all my life. It's been feel, feel, feel, go, go, go. But suddenly I see the glowing entrances to five, six, maybe three hundred paths. It's confusing me, the sight of them all, all the ways this can go. *Bird Box* somehow being dropped. *Bird Box* featured on *Good Morning America*. *Bird Box* atop the *New York*

Times bestseller list. *Bird Box* selling one copy. I see myself at literary parties; I see myself drinking at the Blarney Stone again. I see myself in another hallway. Always another army cot in another hallway.

"At least we got to play," the woman says.

Yes, the pool table. At the Blarney Stone. A table I once stood on and—

"Oh my God, Allison," I say.

I don't care if these people hear me now. In fact, I suddenly want an audience. An auditorium.

Because, suddenly, just as suddenly as the night having ended inside, *I've got it.*

The answer: so natural, so obvious. Phenomenological. As if the question had been asked weeks ago *because* I was supposed to figure it out tonight, *this* night, the night we watched *The Evil Dead.*

"Okay," I say. "Okay, check this out . . ."

The panic and anxiety are ebbing, replaced molecule by molecule with a certainty I haven't felt in a long time.

"What is this, a thriller?" Allison says. "Tell me how it ends."

I stop pacing. I step into the porch light, facing her.

"What's being undervalued here, what's being underestimated, is the *writing of the book itself.*"

"I don't think you've underestimated that all night. Or ever, for that matter."

"Right. And that's just it. This is why the question has

nagged me for so long. It's why I felt like I had to answer it. Because I *could*. And I *can*. What the artist deserves . . . is the work of art itself."

"Go on."

I step closer to her. The panic and anxiety are far from me now.

"When we say *the artist only deserves the work of art,* it's the word *only* that's throwing us off. It's making the book or song sound like a consolation prize. Like, Hey kid, you tried. But at least you still got the book. Right? Right. Except . . . *except* for the fact that the book, and the writing of the book, is literally the most elevated, exciting, rewarding, cathartic, brilliant experience I've ever known. And here I am . . . asking myself what the artist deserves? But hasn't he or she already been *given* the greatest experience, the greatest feeling, they'll ever get by writing it? Yes. And so, the reason the question was so fucking vexing is not because it's complicated, it's because the answer is *in* the question itself. The *artist*. And you can't be an artist unless you finish works of art. This means we've been asking ourselves: What does the man or woman deserve who has already received everything? And here we've struggled to answer because it's like asking how much more water should we put into a glass that's already full."

Bats flutter above us. I hear the couple in the alley, listening to us, to me.

"The artist deserves the work of art. And the experience of creating it. These other things . . . none of them compare to the satisfaction, the fulfillment, of writing the book itself. All my energy, all the momentum I get from the writing is put back *into* the writing. Finish a rough draft to feel good enough to rewrite it. Rewrite it to feel confident enough to write a second book. And on we go. The artist deserves the work of art itself. There's no 'only' about it."

I will discover this in full over the course of the next ten years. I will experience firsthand how true this is. Even if I already knew it.

"But it's not really a revelation," I say. "That's the wild part. This is all something we already know. You and me. We already live this way and have lived this way our entire lives. Any inner peace, any confidence, peace of mind, satisfaction . . . I've never played a show that beat the writing of the song. Or . . . maybe what I mean to say is this: Let's say me and Frank N. Stein are getting a drink together. We both have movie deals. He tells me how unbelievably excited he is about the fact he has a movie deal. And I . . . I feel the same way he does. About *that*. It's unbelievable. It's incredible. It's a dream. Yet . . . despite us both feeling the same amount of joy for the same exact thing . . . I know of something that makes you feel . . . *even better.* So rather than lowering the value of a movie deal, of good reviews, of notoriety . . . I'm saying we raise up the experience of creating the work of art itself. Too many people talk about how hard it is, how painful, the sacrifice. And yes, okay, this is all true . . . but the payoff is unparalleled.

It's when you know you have expressed yourself in full. *That's* what the artist deserves, Allison. *The work of art.*"

Some laughter from the alley.

"Sounds good, brother!" the man calls.

"You two rule!" the woman yells.

Then they walk off and Allison and I are kissing again and this time it feels like it's going to lead somewhere else.

We kiss our way up the back porch steps, through the back door, through the kitchen, into the living room, onto the couch. I'm thinking of the bathroom in the building where Sam Raimi and Bruce Campbell were trying to shop this masterpiece of a moving painting we watched tonight. It's dark in here and I half expect Allison to suddenly start cackling in a demon voice. I kinda want her to. Allison in a Michigan State sweatshirt, telling me she's going to swallow my soul.

But . . .

"Breadcrumbs," I say. "And the body of work. And how we leave ourselves presents . . ."

"No words," Allison says. "No body of work. Just bodies . . ."

But I'm still thinking as the two of us start making out on a couch only slightly wider than the army cot we once slept on, in the days we first met, still not long ago at all. I'm thinking of the book deal I got mere months after meeting her and how Allison has always felt like the gears shifting into place for me, like meeting her started something more powerful than anything I'd known before her.

"It's not a matter of being optimistic," I tell her. "It's being in love. There's a difference."

"No words."

"Is there such a thing as bad love?"

"You're still using words."

"Good, bad, it's all love."

And I start hearing that drummer. In the dark of Rose and Kenickie's place I hear the invisible drummer sitting down on her stool, picking up her sticks, pounding a few bass drum hits, softly, getting ready to play. She's adjusting things, there's time for me to make it back to the office before she starts playing a full beat. She's putting cheese-cloth on the toms. Tuning the snare.

"I love you," I say.

But we're not talking anymore.

Not for many minutes.

And I feel like we're still in the bathroom of the *Evil Dead* building, and maybe we always will be.

After, we fall asleep side by side in a space not necessarily big enough for one. I dream of hands tightening cymbal stands. A distant roll of a snare.

Preparing . . .

Home. Calling.

And the beating of the body of work.

Years later, I will see this night as the one in which I articulated something I'd long vaguely felt. The night in which I finally voiced my gratitude to the writer's life.

I'll forever see it as one radiant night along the phenomenological path, with breadcrumbs fanning out far behind it. I will see the two of us, Allison and me, sleeping on that couch, the two of us a little brighter than the dark.

Maybe we're sleeping in a cabin in Tennessee.

And maybe we got there in a yellow car.

And it will be a place I will want to return to, that night, a place I will bring up many times. Many times I'll bring up the night we watched *The Evil Dead*. I'll say it had everything: young love, dying love, the arcs of passion, the fear of a coming career, the galvanizing of certain philosophies for having had the chance to speak them out loud. I will remind Allison, too, that she showed me the movie as much as I showed her. And I will forever grasp the energy the four of us created that night. I'll keep it behind glass.

Where it deserves to be.

But first . . . we sleep.

Me and Allison. Allison and me.

And the breadcrumbs prove we were there.

Then . . .

We wake. And we feel a little insane. And we sit up on the edge of the couch and we hold our heads a good long while before deciding to leave. Allison sees the bottle of tequila and holds out her hand to hide it from sight. I get up and use the bathroom and I don't see Raoul in the mirror. I don't see that party from New York City anywhere in the glass.

But I do see the evidence of a shower, just taken. Either

Kenickie or Rose must've already got up and left the house. And I wonder (how could I not?) if we met up with them on the last night they'd ever share. I think of the two of them, cuddled on a couch. No doubt they once shared the very one Allison and I did last night. I picture them watching a movie together, long before the night we showed up, something scary, the two of them alone in the house, high and drunk, laughing hysterically, making out as one movie became two, two then three. Kenickie and Rose were somewhere further back on the arc then, when they were still somewhere between young love and dying love, far enough away from both not to consider either at all.

When I exit the bathroom, Allison is standing, half-smiling, laughing at how insane we both feel. I try to take a picture of her with my memory, wanting the picture for reference, wanting always to be able to look at this picture, and I never want us to look any different from the way we do then, the morning after watching *Evil Dead*.

We don't actually see Kenickie or Rose as we step out of their house, but we leave a note, thanking them for having us.

On the walk to the car, I hear the drummer has started playing. A simple, straight beat. I tell her I'm on my way.

I fumble for the keys.

"Shit, am I still drunk?" I say.

"Don't say *drunk*. Gonna make me sick."

We get in the car. We pause before starting the engine. We sit in silence.

The sun is brutal.

"Maybe we should take it easy tonight," Allison says.

I start the car.

"I don't know," I say, pulling away from the curb. The motion makes us both wince. "I was thinking *Army of Darkness*."

"You really are gonna make me puke."

We pass the Blarney Stone, reach Woodward again.

As we're pulling onto Detroit's main road, Allison says, "I know you're gonna want to talk the whole way back. So, give me one word that describes the whole night. And that'll do for now. And let's stop for food on the way."

"One word."

"Yes."

I pull onto Woodward.

I smile.

"Eudaemonia."

Acknowledgments

If you've just finished this book, then you've spent many pages with my actual voice, and so I'll keep this brief:

The truth is, I don't feel right calling people "my team." Agent Kristin Nelson is no more "my team" than I am hers. We're in this book thing *together.* The same goes for editor Tricia Narwani and Del Rey Books, Penguin Random House. We're all . . . *of a piece.* A think tank, a brain trust.

A team.

Kristin, Tricia, Ryan Lewis, Wayne Alexander, Ayesha Shibli, Keith Clayton, Scott Shannon, Alex Larned, Julie Leung, Marcelle Iten Busto, Ada Maduka, David Moench, Sabrina Shen, Ashleigh Heaton, Kay Popple, Cindy Berman, Paul Gilbert, Rachelle Mandik, Angela McNally, Diane Hobbing . . . it's wonderful to me that this group of people got behind this particular story, unlike any we'd done before.

But that just underscores what I already knew, doesn't it?

All the people I work with, play with, talk with daily . . . they all love the same thing I do.

We all love *books*.

(And a special thank-you to Dave Simmer, always.)

About the Author

JOSH MALERMAN is a *New York Times* bestselling author and one of two singer-songwriters for the rock band the High Strung. His debut novel, *Bird Box,* was the inspiration for the hit Netflix film of the same name. His other novels include *Daphne, Pearl, Spin a Black Yarn,* and *Malorie,* the sequel to *Bird Box.* Malerman lives in Michigan with his fiancée, the artist-musician Allison Laakko.

joshmalerman.com
X: @JoshMalerman
facebook.com/JoshMalerman
Instagram: @joshmalerman

About the Type

This book was set in Sabon, a typeface designed by the well-known German typographer Jan Tschichold (1902–74). Sabon's design is based upon the original letterforms of sixteenth-century French type designer Claude Garamond and was created specifically to be used for three sources: foundry type for hand composition, Linotype, and Monotype. Tschichold named his typeface for the famous Frankfurt typefounder Jacques Sabon (c. 1520–80).